THE OFFICIAL
LICENSE
PLATE BOOK 2002

A COMPLETE PLATE IDENTIFICATION RESOURCE

License Plates
U.S.A., Canada & Mexico

A COLOR REGISTRY OF SPECIAL
PLATES INCLUDING NASCAR®

by Thomson C. Murray

designed by William L Cummings
graphic design by
Chrisan Mohan

ISBN 1-886777-04-7

INTERSTATE DIRECTORY PUBLISHING CO. INC.
220 Cleft Road,
Mill Neck, NY 11765
1-800-347-0473 or 516-922-7160 Fax 6605
www.idpubco.com

The author wishes to thank Larry Greenberg and The American Association of Motor Vehicle Administrators for their help both with this and previous editions. The Motor Vehicle Departments of all 51 U.S and 13 Canadian jurisdictions have been wonderful this year as in the past. A word of appreciation to the Turtle Mountain Tribal Council for granting permission to include their plate. A special word of thanks is due to all my friends at 3M Corporation, the firm who developed the reflective sheeting that makes all these beautiful graphic plates possible.

A special appreciation to: my fellow members of ALPCA including: Alfonso Baca, Michael Wiener, John Northup, David R. Wilson, Chuck Sakryd, Andrew Apgar, Keith Marvin,Don Merrill, Mike McEnaney, Mike Natale, Donald Stow, Arlene Jang, Bob Bittner, Jim Fox, Dave Fraser, Darrell Dady, Kit Sage, Rich Bell,and Richard Dragon.Other key contributors are Chrisan Mohan, Bill Cummings, Jon Goldstein, Chris Kelly, Jim Walton, Goerge Barnes, Jeff Gould, and Barbara Cooney ... all part of the very special team that makes this book and ID Pubco possible.

Dedicated to
Mary Thompson Murray
lovingly remembered as

Geggie

The license plates illustrated in this book are a representative sample selected by the author. They illustrate a typical type of plate issued by a jurisdiction. If the alpha and/or numeric characters duplicate a particular plate currently in use it is strictly coincidental. The material in this book was compiled from information provided by Motor Vehicle authorities. Interstate Directory Publishing Company Inc. is not responsible for any inadvertent inaccuracies or omissions.

ISBN 1-886777-04- 7

Introduction

License plates often have hidden meanings that can be recognized by law enforcement, serious collectors and motor vehicle authorities. This book explains how states and provinces code their plates so you, like the authorities, will be able to look at a plate and tell such things as:

In what county a vehicle is registered
    Occupation of the owner
        Special plates and what they mean
            Age, weight and vehicle use restrictions
                State, City, Federal Government, Diplomatic codes
            Indian tribes

Also:
Addresses and phone numbers for all motor vehicle departments Web Sites are listed.

How to "read" a license plate

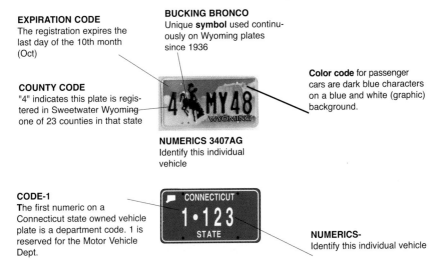

EXPIRATION CODE
The registration expires the last day of the 10th month (Oct)

BUCKING BRONCO
Unique **symbol** used continuously on Wyoming plates since 1936

Color code for passenger cars are dark blue characters on a blue and white (graphic) background.

COUNTY CODE
"4" indicates this plate is registered in Sweetwater Wyoming one of 23 counties in that state

NUMERICS 3407AG
Identify this individual vehicle

CODE-1
The first numeric on a Connecticut state owned vehicle plate is a department code. 1 is reserved for the Motor Vehicle Dept.

NUMERICS-
Identify this individual vehicle

Many States issue special license plates look for these colorful graphic designs.

LICENSE PLATES AND HOW TO READ THEM

The popular name for the metal plate affixed to a vehicle is a "license plate." In many states, particularly in the South, these are commonly referred to as "license tags." Actually the vehicle is not licensed, the driver is. Every vehicle is "registered" with authorities, and the metal plate is issued to identify each particular vehicle and indicate that it has met certain conditions and the owner has paid required registration fees and taxes. The driver is "licensed" and the metal plate is a "registration plate," but for over ninety years the public has used the term "license plate" and we won't try to correct this now.

License plates are issued to indicate proper registration of a vehicle. They also often contain codes which can tell you a lot about the vehicle and the owner. In fact there is an incredible "hidden language" of license plates which this book has been designed to explain.

Although every state and provincial motor vehicle administration uses a different system to issue plates and assign numbers, they all recognize the need for law enforcement authorities to distinguish classes of vehicles by simply glancing at the plate. There are three methods to make these distinctions:

COLOR- Different combinations are used for classes of vehicles.
CAPTIONS- Words are embossed or screen-printed to give special information
CODES- Series of letters and numbers (alpha, numeric characters) used in the plate numbering system that are reserved for special identification

The material in this book has been gathered from Motor Vehicle administrations of all 50 states, District of Columbia, 12 Canadian provinces and territories as well as contributions from members of Automobile License Plate Collectors Association (ALPCA). It is organized to explain how every jurisdiction (state or province) uses these three methods to help authorities "read" a license plate and instantly tell if it is a valid registration, what county it comes from, its weight class, and/or use restrictions, the driver's occupation, and any other special information that may be available about the owner and his vehicle.

PASSENGER CARS

All U.S. and Canadian jurisdictions currently issue permanent or semi-permanent license plates that are used for a number of years and revalidated with decals or windshield decals. Of the 51 U.S. jurisdictions, 32 issue two plates, while the remaining 19 require only one plate per vehicle. The things to look for on license plates are:

COUNTY CODES
OCCUPATION CODES
EXPIRATION CODES
GOVERNMENT DEPARTMENT CODES
CODES RESERVED FOR SPECIAL GROUPS AND OFFICIALS

In many states you can tell in which county a vehicle is registered, if the owner is a member of a special group or organization, and the age and weight of the vehicle. All this information and much more is available from just looking at a license plate and referring to this book.

TRUCKS TRAILERS AND OTHER HEAVY VEHICLES

Trucks, truck tractors, buses, trailers and other heavy vehicles, unlike private passenger cars, must pay a variety of taxes based on weight, miles driven and fuel consumption in addition to registration fees.This is why commercial license plates are often a different color and sometimes changed more frequently than passenger plates.

Every state has at least two sources of revenue that is collected from commercial vehicles: registration fees and fuel consumption taxes. Some states have a third level of taxation based on a formula of miles run and tons carried.

In addition to a registration license plate, a commercial vehicle operating only within the state where it is registered must display a decal or plate showing registration for the payment of fuel and any other taxes required by the particular state. This is usually done by a small plate issued by the Public Service Commission (PSC) or Tax Commissioner, or by a decal on the cab or bumper of the vehicle.

VEHICLES OPERATING INTERSTATE

Private passenger cars can cross state lines and drive freely anywhere within the United States because every state has agreed to honor the registration of a passenger vehicle registered in every other state. This is called full reciprocity.

Commercial vehicles do not enjoy this same freedom of movement over state lines.

States rely heavily on commercial vehicle registration and tax revenue to defray the cost of highway construction and maintenance. They insist that all trucks and other heavy vehicles using their highways pay their fair share. As a result, a commercial or heavy vehicle cannot operate in another state unless there is some agreement between the two states providing for reciprocity (sharing of registration fees). This sharing of registration and tax revenue is called apportionment or proration.

Currently most states have some sort of agreement with every other state to grant full reciprocity or share registration fees and tax revenue based on actual highway use. This is a complicated problem and difficult for both state authorities and the trucking industry to administer and enforce. This situation is one reason you often see multiple plates and decals on vehicles operating interstate .

In recent years 48 states and Alberta, British Columbia, and Saskatchewan have joined the International Registration Plan (IRP) where only one license plate captioned APPORTIONED is issued by the state where the vehicle is based. This is the only plate that has to be displayed by heavy vehicles operating interstate within the member states.

PLATES AND PARKING FOR THE DISABLED

The automobile gives a disabled person in the United States the chance to enjoy independence and mobility.They are given special parking privileges, and every effort is made to meet their needs and still not inconvenience the general public.

The familiar wheelchair symbol is used worldwide. The official name of this symbol is International Symbol of Access (ISA) and appears on signs, placards and license plates to identify vehicles transporting disabled persons and the parking areas reserved for their use.

Until 1991 there were no uniform guidelines covering the administration of special parking for the disabled. Every state handled the situation in their individual manner. Some of the problems are abuse of special parking by unauthorized people using disabled plates and special parking plates designed and issued in one state were often not recognized or honored in other states. The Department of Transportation (DOT) developed a uniform system for disabled parking which became federal law March 11, 1991. Under this law every qualified applicant for special parking privileges will have the choice of either a special plate embossed with the ISA or a parking placard to hang from the rearview mirror on the inside of the vehicle. The advantage of the placard is it can be moved to any vehicle, and the car remains unmarked when the placard is not displayed. The law also permits two placards to be issued to one individual if needed.

Blue placards are issued only for permanent disability and are renewed periodically by the issuing jurisdiction.

Red placards are issued for temporary disabilities and are valid for a maximum period of six months.

These representative samples of disabled persons parking permits from two jurisdictions (Washington and Montana) were provided through the courtesy of:

The American Association of Motor Vehicle Administrators, Arlington VA

Actual size of placard is 3 1/2 x 9 1/4 in.

Temporary License Plates

Documents printed on paper or cardboard are attached to newly registered vehicles as temporary identification until a metal plate is available. The size, design, color and the materials used for these temporary license plates varies widely between jurisdictions. AAMVA working with OPSEC CORP. has developed a secure temporary tag that is designed to prevent alteration and counterfeiting. The AAMVA secure temporary tag system is currently used is 15 states. The secure tag uses a hologram strip and a write-resistant overlay where type will disappear if and when it is altered.

Size
6 X 12"

permit

The AAMVA temporary license plate system is used in the following states:
AZ, CO, DC, GA, IL, IN, KY, MD, NJ, NM, OH, PA, VA, WV, WY.

DIPLOMATIC LICENSE PLATES

In 1985 the United States Department of State began issuing red white and blue plates to vehicles owned by foreign missions. Prefix **C,D,S** is used nationwide, suffix **A,C,D,S** is reserved for The United Nations.The 2 letters used in the numbering system is a country code.

AA	CONGO	**FP**	MOROCCO	**KX**	SUDAN	
AC	IVORY COAST	**FR**	PHILIPPINES	**LC**	VENEZUELA	
AF	JAPAN	**FS**	NETHERLANDS	**LG**	TURKEY	
AH	MADAGASCAR	**FT**	QATAR	**LD**	VIET NAM	
AJ	PANAMA	**FV**	SRI LANKA	**LH**	ISRAEL	
AK	CAPE VERDE	**FW**	VATICAN	**LJ**	ISRAEL	
AQ	SYRIA	**FX**	SIERRA LEONE	**LK**	DEL. TO EEC	
AU	UGANDA	**FY**	SOUTH AFRICA	**LW**	GERMANY	
AV	ISRAEL	**FZ**	SURINAME	**MK**	DJIBOUTI	
AW	ORG. OF AFRICAN UNITY	**GC**	SWEDEN	**ML**	DIEGO GARCIA	
BL	SOUTH AFRICA	**GD**	UKRAINE	**MN**	COMOROS	
BY	SOLOMON ISLANDS	**GG**	ZAMBIA	**MP**	BAHAMAS	
BZ	IRAQ	**GM**	TURKEY	**MQ**	MONACO	
CB	CAMBODIA	**GP**	ALBANIA	**MW**	MALDIVES	
CC	ETHIOPIA	**GQ**	NORTH KOREA	**NA**	OMAN	
CS	AFGHANISTAN	**HL**	ST. LUCIA	**NB**	NEW GUINEA	
CT	BHUTAN	**HN**	MONGOLIA	**NC**	PARAGUAY	
CU	BOTSWANA	**HV**	BELGIUM	**ND**	ROMANIA	
CV	BURMA	**HW**	GUATEMALA	**NQ**	ANGOLA	
CW	CAMEROON	**HX**	BENIN	**PA**	AUSTRIA	
CX	BURUNDI	**HY**	GUINEA BISSAU	**PB**	BARBADOS	
CY	CHINA	**HZ**	HAITI	**PC**	BELIZE	
DA	COLOMBIA	**JB**	HONDURAS	**PD**	BERMUDA	
DB	COSTA RICA	**JC**	KUWAIT	**PF**	BOLIVIA	
DC	CUBA	**JD**	MAURITIUS	**PG**	BYELORUSSIA	
DD	CYPRUS	**JF**	NIGERIA	**PH**	CZECH.	
DF	DOM. REP	**JG**	PORTUGAL	**PI**	ISRAEL	
DG	ECUADOR	**JH**	SOMALIA	**PK**	NORWAY	
DH	FR. CARIBBEAN	**JJ**	CHAD	**PL**	CHILE	
DI	ISRAEL.	**JK**	TURKEY	**PM**	BRUNEI	
DJ	FRANCE	**JM**	YUGOSLAVIA	**PR**	ARGENTINA	
DK	GREECE	**JP**	TUNISIA	**PS**	ZIMBABWE	
DL	INDIA	**JQ**	TOGO	**PV**	ZAIRE	
DM	IRAN	**KG**	EQU.GUINEA	**QA**	N. YEMEN	
DN	DENMARK	**KH**	HUNGARY	**QD**	BURKINA FASO	
DP	BANGLADESH	**KJ**	LITHUANIA	**QL**	ST. KITTS	
FC	FORMER USSR	**KK**	FIJI	**QM**	BULGARIA	
FF	ANTIGUA	**KL**	JORDAN	**QN**	LAOS	
FG	CEN.AF.REP.	**KM**	JAMAICA	**QP**	LATVIA	
FH	IRELAND	**KN**	GABON	**QQ**	LESOTHO	
FI	ISRAEL	**KP**	LUXEMBOURG	**QR**	MALAWI	
FJ	LEBANON	**KR**	MALAYSIA	**QS**	MOZAMBIQUE	
FK	KENYA	**KS**	MEXICO	**QT**	NEW ZEALAND	
FL	LIBERIA	**KT**	NAMIBIA	**QU**	NICARAGUA	
FM	LIBYA	**KU**	SAO TOME / PRINCIPE	**QV**	NIGER	
FN	MALTA	**KV**	SAUDI ARABIA	**QW**	POLAND	
		KW	SEYCHELLES	**QX**	PAKISTAN	
				QY	S. YEMEN	

QZ	INDONESIA
RB	RWANDA
RC	ST VINCENT
RD	SENEGAL
RL	URUGUAY
SG	ISRAEL
ST	DOMINICA
SX	USSR
TC	MALI
TF	ALGERIA
TG	CANADA
TH	EGYPT
TJ	GERMANY
TK	NETH. ANTIL.
TL	EL SALVADOR
TM	ICELAND
TN	NEPAL
TP	MAURITANIA
TR	ITALY
TS	IRAQ
TT	GUYANA
TU	GUINEA
TV	GHANA
TW	GAMBIA
TX	FINLAND
TY	GRENADA
TZ	PERU
UA	BAHRAIN
UF	ESTONIA
UH	SPAIN
UX	TRINIDAD & TOBAGO
VF	THAILAND
VG	TANZANIA
VH	SWITZERLAND
VJ	BRAZIL
VK	SINGAPORE
VL	SWAZILAND
WB	U.A.E.
WD	S KOREA
WM	W. SAMOA
WZ	UNIT. KNGDM
XF	TURKEY
XZ	AUSTRALIA
YM	HONG KONG

UNITED STATES GOVERNMENT VEHICLES

The General Services Administration (GSA) maintains vehicles in motor pools across the country for official use of Government agencies and departments. All plates are blue on white. The prefix indicates vehicle type.

G11 - Sedans; intermediate; subcompact
G12 - Sedans; compact
G14 - Sedans; standard
G21 - Station wagons; subcompact/ compact
G23 - Station wagons; standard
G31 - Ambulances; buses
G41 - Trucks- cargo 1/2 ton and under (4x2)
G42 - Trucks- cargo 3/4 ton (4x2)
G43 - Trucks- cargo 1 ton (4x2)

G61 - Trucks - cargo 1/2 ton and under (4x4)
G62 - Trucks - cargo 3/4 ton (4x4)
G63 - Trucks - cargo 1 ton (4x4)
G71 - Trucks - cargo 12,500 - 23,999 GVW
G81 - Trucks - cargo 24,000+ GVW gasoline
G82 - Trucks - Cargo 24,000+ GVW diesel
G91 - Trucks, trailers , semi-trailers (special purpose type vehicles)

Federal Government owned vehicles owned by individual departments can be identified by the alpha prefix code as follows:

A - Agriculture
ACT - Action
AF - Air Force
C - Commerce
CA - Civil Aeronautics Board
CE - Corps of Engineers
CPSC - Consumer Product Safety Comm.
CS - Civil Service Commission
D - Defense
DA - Defense Contract Audit Agency
DOT - Dept. of Transportation
DA - Defense Supply Agency
E - Energy Research & Development Admin.
EO - Executive Office of the President
  Council of Economic Advisors
  National Security Council
  Office of Management & Budget
EPA - Environmental Protection Agency
EPS - Executive Protection Services
FA - Federal Aviation Administration
FC - Federal Communications Comm.
FD - Federal Deposit Insurance Corp.
FM - Federal Mediation &Conciliation Serv.
FP - Federal Power Commission
FR - Federal Reserve System
FT - Federal Trade Commission
G - Interagency Motor Pool System
GA - General Accounting Office
GP - Government Printing Office
GS - General Services Administration
H - Housing & Urban Development
HW - Health, Education & Welfare

I - Interior
IA - Information Agency
IBC- International Boundary Commission
IC - Interstate Commerce Commission
J - Justice
JB - Judicial Branch
L - Labor
LA - D of C Redevelopment Land Agency
LB - Legislative Branch
N - Navy
NA - Nat'l. Aeronautics & Space Admin.
NG - National Guard Bureau
NH - Nat'l Cap. Housing Authority
NL - National Labor Relations Board
NP - Nat'l Cap. Planning Comm.
NRC - Nuclear Regulatory Comm.
NS - National Science Commission
OEO - Office Economic Opportunity
P - Postal Service
PC -Panama Canal Company
RB - Renegotiation Board
RR - Railroad Retirement Board
S - State Department
SB - Small Business Administration
SE - Securities & Exchange Commission
SH - Soldiers & Sailor"s Home
SI - Smithsonian Institution Ntl Gallery Art.
T - Treasury
TV - Tennessee Valley Authority
VA - Veterans Administration,
  W - Army

SAMPLE LICENSE PLATES

A good way to begin a license plate collection is to order a sample plate from each state and province.This book lists the address of every Motor Vehicle Department. If you write them, they will often send you a sample plate for a modest fee. These fees may change.

ALABAMA- $ 3.00
ALASKA- $ 3.00
ARIZONA-$ *6.50
ARKANSAS-** FREE
CALIFORNIA- $12.00
COLORADO- $ 3.00
CONNECTICUT- $ 5.00
DELAWARE- $ 7.00
FLORIDA- FREE
GEORGIA-NO samples
HAWAII-$ 10.00
IDAHO- $ 12.00
ILLINOIS-$ 3.00
INDIANA-$ *4.00
IOWA- $ 3.00
KANSAS- $ 5.50
KENTUCKY- $ 5.00
LOUISIANA-$ 9.50
MAINE-$ 5.00
MARYLAND - FREE
MASSACHUSETTS - $10.00
MICHIGAN- $ 5.00
MINNESOTA- $ 3.00
MISSISSIPPI-$2.00
MISSOURI-$ 7.50
MONTANA- $ 7.50
NEBRASKA- $ 5.00
NEVADA- $ 2.00
NEW HAMPSHIRE- $ 5.00
NEW JERSEY- $ 5.00
NEW MEXICO- $ 5.00
NEW YORK- NO SAMPLES
NORTH CAROLINA- $ 10.00
NORTH DAKOTA- $ 5.00
OHIO - FREE
OKLAHOMA- $ 2.00
OREGON- $ 2.50
PENNSYLVANIA- $ 5.00
RHODE ISLAND - $ 2.00
SOUTH CAROLINA - $ 10.00
SOUTH DAKOTA - *$ 3.00
TENNESSEE- FREE
TEXAS- $ 6.90
UTAH - $ 5.00
VERMONT - $ 10.00
VIRGINIA - $ 10.00
WASHINGTON-** FREE
WEST VIRGINIA- $ 5.00
WISCONSIN - $ 2.00
WYOMING - $ 2.50
*Includes postage cost
**expired plate available

CANADA
ALBERTA- $ 10.42 CDN
BRITISH COLUMBIA- $ 10.70 CDN
MANITOBA-FREE
NEW BRUNSWICK- FREE
NEWF.& LAB.- $ 10.00
NORTHWEST TERR.- $ 10.00
NOVA SCOTIA- $ 5.35
ONTARIO- $15.00 CDN
PRINCE ED. ISL.-$ 16.00
QUEBEC- $ 5.00
SASKATCHEWAN- $ 10.00 CDN
YUKON- $ 5.35 CDN

When writing for sample plates it is important to note that policies governing sample plate issuance and pricing can and do change often, It is advisable to send a money order - many jurisdictions do not accept personal checks. Many states offer a variety of passenger and non-passenger sample and/or expired plates as well as expired and sample validation decals.

GUAM
DEPT. OF REVENUE & TAXATION
VEHICLE REGISTRATION BRANCH
855 W MARINE DRIVE
AGANA GU 96910
SAMPLE PLATE $5.00

US VIRGIN ISLANDS
POLICE DEPT, CRIMINAL JUSTICE COMPLEX,
VETERANS DRIVE
CHARLOTTE AMALIE , ST THOMAS VI 00802, ATTN MOTOR VEHICLE BUREAU
SAMPLE PLATE $23.00

DISTRICT OF COLUMBIA-
SAMPLE PLATES ARE NO LONGER AVAILABLE.

ALABAMA

Passenger Plates and Renewal Decals

Front **Rear** **YEAR EXPIRE**
2002   2003

MO ★ Stars Fell On ★ YR
3AA001A
Alabama

2002 ALA   **2003** ALA

Alabama issues one fully- reflectorized license plate to all vehicles, a new **STARS FELL ON ALABAMA** design is issued beginning Jan 01, 2002. New Truck plates are issued every year.

Passenger Plates

★ Stars Fell On ★
3AA001A
Alabama

New Hi Dixie
25AA123
Alabama

★ Stars Fell On ★
DIXIE
Alabama

★ Stars Fell On ★
& **18100**
Alabama

Passenger regular   Older issue valid 02   Personalized   Disabled

♥ Alabama ·
17700 MU
· MUNICIPAL ·

★ ALABAMA ★
NR4Z
· AMATEUR RADIO ·

Alabama ♥
D 12345
NOV DEALER 2003

State owned   Amateur Radio   Dealer

Truck and trailer plate

♥ *Alabama* ♥
1X10001
NOV   2002

♥ *Alabama* ♥
TR10001
NOV   2000

★ ALABAMA ★
X8 50556
APPORTIONED 2002

♥ *Alabama* ♥
123 456
NOV APPORTIONED 2003

Truck Annual   Trailer   Apportioned Truck 2002 Expire   Apportioned Truck 2003 Expire

Temporary Permit

Dealers and county offices issue a 20 day paper permit (6x12") validated by pen.

ALABAMA TWENTY DAY TEMPORARY TAG
ISSUED IN CONJUNCTION WITH A TEMPORARY TAG RECEIPT
EXPIRES
19 **A316701**
MONTH DAY YEAR
ISSUED TO:
ISSUED FOR:
ISSUED BY:

permit

Special Plates

Colleges and University

ALABAMA
42AU
AUBURN

The University of
12U34
· ALABAMA ·

UNIVERSITY OF
South
SA999
· Alabama ·

TUSKEGEE
UNIVERSITY
TU20H
· Alabama ·

Alburn   Crimson Tide   University of South Alabama   Tuskegee Univ.

· HUNTINGDON ·
COLLEGE
HC500
· Alabama ·

JACKSONVILLE
STATE UNIVERSITY
J1400
· Alabama ·

TROY STATE UNIVERSITY
1000T
· ALABAMA ·

University of Alabama
at Birmingham
UAB **999B**
· Alabama ·

HUNTINGDON   JACKSONVILLE STATE   TROY STATE   BIRMINGHAM

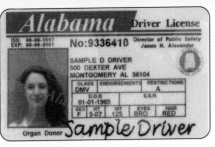

DRIVER LICENSE

POLICE PATCH

Motorcycle

www.dps.state.al.us/
website

Special Plates

Military Plates / Optional Graphics

Nuclear Veteran

Disabled Veteran

Active Reserve

WW II Veteran

Sheaksphere

Environment

Ham Radio

Wildlife

Helping Schools

Children's Trust

Alabama Cattlemen

Forest Bird

Alabama plates have a numeric county prefix. The counties and (county seats) are:

1. Jefferson (Birmingham)
2. Mobile (Mobile)
3. Montgomery (Montgomery)
4. Autauga (Prattville)
5. Baldwin (Bay Minette)
6. Barbour (Clayton)
7. Bibb (Centreville)
8. Blount (Oneonta)
9. Bullock (Union Springs)
10. Butler (Greenville)
11. Calhoun (Anniston)
12. Chambers (Lafayette)
13. Cherokee (Centre)
14. Chilton (Clanton)
15. Choctaw (Butler)
16. Clarke (Grove Hill)
17. Clay (Ashland)
18. Cleburne (Heflin)
19. Coffee (Elba)
20. Colbert (Tuscumbia)
21. Conecuh (Evergreen)
22. Coosa (Rockford)
23. Covington (Andalusia)

24. Crenshaw (Luverne)
25. Cullman (Cullman)
26. Dale (Ozark)
27. Dallas (Selma)
28. DeKalb (Fort Payne)
29. Elmore (Wetumpka)
30. Escambia (Brewton)
31. Etowah (Gadsden)
32. Fayette (Fayette)
33. Franklin (Russellville)
34. Geneva (Geneva)
35. Greene (Eutaw)
36. Hale (Greensboro)
37. Henry (Abbeville)
38. Houston (Dothan)
39. Jackson (Scottsboro)
40. Lamar (Vernon)
41. Lauderdale (Florence)
42. Lawrence (Moulton)
43. Lee (Opelika)
44. Limestone (Athens)
45. Lowndes (Hayneville)
46. Macon (Tuskegee)

47. Madison (Huntsville)
48. Marengo (Linden)
49. Marion (Hamilton)
50. Marshall (Guntersville)
51. Monroe (Monroeville)
52. Morgan (Decatur)
53. Perry (Marion)
54. Pickens (Carrollton)
55. Pike (Troy)
56. Randolph (Wedowee)
57. Russell (Phenix City)
58. Shelby (Columbiana)
59. Saint. Clair (Ashville)
60. Sumter (Livingston)
61. Talladega (Talladega)
62. Tallapoosa (Dadeville)
63. Tuscaloosa (Tuscaloosa)
64. Walker (Jasper)
65. Washington (Chatom)
66. Wilcox (Camden)
67. Winston (Double Springs)

Alabama Department of Revenue, Division of Motor Vehicles.
50 ripley street, P.O. box 327630, Montgomery, Al 36132 Tel. 334-242-9000

ALASKA

Passenger Plates and Renewal Decals

Front	Rear	YEAR EXPIRE	
		2002	2003

Front
·ALASKA·
DBA 123
• The Last Frontier •

Rear
MO ·ALASKA· YR
DBA 123
• The Last Frontier •

2002
G070828
02

2003
G070828
03

"The Last Frontier" issues two fully-reflectorized license plates. A three alpha- three numeric format is used for all regular plates.

Passenger Plates

·ALASKA·
DBA 123
• The Last Frontier •

Passenger regular

·ALASKA·
ICEBOX
• The Last Frontier •

Personalized

·ALASKA·
HCP♿123
• HANDICAPPED •

Handicapped

MO ·ALASKA· YR
FWP 123
• PROTECTION •

Fish and Wildlife Protection

·ALASKA·
1001BA
• •

Truck

·ALASKA·
1001SA
• COMMERCIAL •

Trailer

Temporary Permit

Alaska DMV officers and dealers issue temporary operating permits to new and used vehicle owners while registration is processed. Permit are displayed on rear window validated by marking pen.

EXPIRES _____
ALASKA TEMPORARY PERMIT
M 388853
SERIAL NO _____ YEAR MAKE MODEL
DATE OF ISSUE _____ ISSUE BY

permit

Special Plates

·ALASKA·
KENAI
The Last Frontier

Optional Graphic Caribou

MO ALASKA YR
Gold Rush
123 ABC
Centennial

Optional Graphic Gold Rush

· ALASKA ·
PWS◯123
Prince William Sound
Community Police

College

· ALASKA ·
Help Keep Alaska's Children Safe and Healthy
KID 224

Support Children

MO ·ALASKA· YR
VMC 123
• VETERAN •

Marine Veteran

·ALASKA·
DAV♿123
DISABLED VETERAN

Disabled Veteran

·ALASKA·
POW055
EX PRISONER OF WAR

Former POW

· ALASKA ·
VMC 123
• NATIONAL GUARD •

Nat. Guard

12

DRIVER LICENSE

POLICE PATCH

Motorcycle

AK

www.state.ak.us/bmv/

website

Special Plates

Pearl Harbor Survivor

Tribal Issue

Tribal Issue

Tribal Issue

Alaska Department of Administration, Division of Motor Vehicles.
2150 Dowling Road, Anchorage, AK 99507   Tel. 907-269-5559

13

ARKANSAS

Passenger Plates and Renewal Decals

Front   **Rear**   **YEAR EXPIRE**

2002   2003

"**The Natural State**" issues one fully-reflectorized plate for passenger vehicles. Many of the non-passenger and annual plates are not reflectorized.

Passenger Plates

Passenger regular

Older issue valid 02

Personalized

Personalized

Disabled

City Owned

Truck and trailer plates

Truck

Semi-Trailer

Apportioned Truck

Apportioned Truck

Temporary Permits

ARKANSAS dealers can issue paperboard drive out and transit permits validated by marking pen.

DRIVER LICENSE

POLICE PATCH

Motorcycle

AR

www.state.ar.us/dfa/
index.html
website

Special Plates

College

Orphanage Bus

Antique

Wildlife

Retired Veteran

Reserve

Disabled Vet

Former POW

WW II Vet.

Korean War Vet.

Vietnam Vet.

Persian Gulf Vet.

Purple Heart

Medal of Honor

Justice of Peace

Street Rod

Fire Fighter

Amateur Radio

School

Disabled Vet.

ARIZONA

Passenger Plates and Renewal Decals

Front   Rear   YEAR EXPIRE 2002   2003

AZ **02** 000000 K
EMISSIONS COMPLIANCE

AZ **02** G 000000
NON EMISSIONS

AZ **03** K 000000
EMISSIONS COMPLIANCE

AZ **03** N 000000
NON EMISSIONS

"**The Grand Canyon State**" issues one reflectorized graphic license plate for most vehicles, having dropped the two plate requirement.

Passenger Plates

Passenger regular

Older issue valid 02

Personalized

Disability

Truck Tractor

Truck

Apportioned Truck

Trailer

Manufacturer Test

Manufacturer Test 12M

Manufacturer Test 26M

Manufacturer Test 80M

Temporary Permit

Dealers issue new owners a paperboard temporary plate which is attached to the norml plate area, and validated by marking pen. 6" x 12" one color black on white.

permit

16

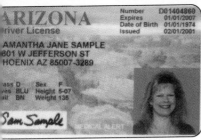

POLICE PATCH

www.dot.state.az.us
website

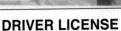

Motorcycle

DRIVER LICENSE

Special Plates

Farm Vehicle

Alternative Fuel

Environment

Transporter

Northern Arizona University

University of Arizona

Arizona State University

University of Arizona

National Guard

Disability Veteran

Purple Heart

Pearl Horbor survivor

Legion of Valor

Medal of Honor

Former POW

Veteran

Fire Fighter

Fraternal order of Police

Amateur Radio

Foreign Consul

Horseless Carriage

Child Abuse prevention

Hearing Impaired

Historic Vehicle

CALIFORNIA

Passenger Plates and Renewal Decals

Front	Rear	YEAR EXPIRE
		2002 2003

California **2ABC123**   MO *California* YR **2ABC123**   🔵 CA 2002 A/C/T L 0000000 M   🔵 CA 2003 A/C/T L 0000000 M

"The Golden State" has not had a complete general plate re-issue since 1963 and five different bases are current in use. Plates are issued in pairs and fully reflectorized.

Passenger Plates

California **2ABC123**
Passenger regular

CALIFORNIA **3A12345**
Passenger 1988 issue

CALIFORNIA **2A12345** The Golden State
Passenger 1987 issue

CALIFORNIA **123 ABC**
Passenger 1970 issue

CALIFORNIA **ABC 123**
Passenger 1963 issue

California **SABAKA**
Personalized

CALIFORNIA Ⓔ**400049**
State Owned

California **66564** D/P ♿
Disabled

California **5M37250**
Commercial Vehicle

MO CALIFORNIA YR **4V80988**
Commercial Vehicle

MO CALIFORNIA YR **3A69400** The Golden State
Commercial Vehicle

CALIFORNIA **1J79500**
Commercial Vehicle

CAL APPORTIONED **SP57323**
App. Power Unit

CAL APPORTIONED **BP34053**
App. Power Unit

CAL APPORTIONED **GT45251**
App. Trailer

CAL APPORTIONED **AT37535**
App. Trailer

Temporary Permit

Dealers issue a small paper permit that is folded to hide the owner's name, but show the VIN number, it is placed on the front windshield.

permit

DMV NEW DEALER NOTICE TEMPORARY IDENTIFACTION
1234567
NAME_____VIN_____

DRIVER LICENSE

POLICE PATCH

www.dmv.ca.gov
website

Motorcycle

Special Plates

California Arts

Lake Tahoe

Yosemite

Coastal Commission

Fire Fighter

Children Fund

Children Fund

Children Fund

Purple Heart

Pearl Harbor Survivor

State Assembly

State Assembly

State Senate

State Senate

Purple Heart

Pearl Harbor Survivor

UCLA

Sesquicentennnial

California Department of Motor Vehicles
2415 First Avenue, Sacramento CA 95818   Tel. 916-657-7667   19

COLORADO

Passenger Plates and Renewal Decals

Front	Rear	YEAR EXPIRE	
		2002	2003

Front

Rear

NON-EMISSION EMISSION NON-EMISSION EMISSIO

Colorado issues two reflectorized green and white mountain scene passenger plates to passenger vehicles, older design plates had a 2 - 3 alpha county code prefix.

Passenger Plates

Passenger regular	Passenger Older Issue	Passenger Older Issue	Personalized

Disabled	City Owned	County Owned	Designer Plate

Truck and trailer plate

Truck	Apportioned Truck	Apportioned Trailer	Permanent Truck

GVW Truck	GVW Truck

Temporary Permit

Licensed dealers county clerks, recorders and DMV issue a paper temporary registration permit (8 $\frac{1}{2}$ x 5 $\frac{1}{2}$) validated by pen. It has a security hologram.

permit

DRIVER LICENSE

POLICE PATCH

Motorcycle

Special Plates

College

Pers.onlized optional Graphic

Veteran

Pioneer

Purple Heart

Former POW

Collector

10TH MTN DIV.

Medal of Honor

National Guard

Pearl Harbor Servivor

Member of Congress

Agriculture

WildLife

Collector

Colorado Department of Revenue Motor Vehicle Division
1881 Pierce Street, Lakewood, CO 80214   Tel. 303-205-5600

CONNECTICUT
Passenger Plates and Renewal Decals

Front	Rear	YEAR EXPIRE	
		2002	**2003**

APR 2002 CT000403   **APR 2003** CT000403

"The Constitution State" issues two fully-reflectorized plates to all passenger vehicles

Passenger regular

Older issue valid 02

Personalized

Personalized

State owned

Disabled

Truck and trailer plate

Truck

Trailer

Apportioned Truck

Apportioned Trailer

COMBINATION

COMBINATION

Temporary Permit

Cardboard temporary plates (6 x11") are issued by DMV Expiration dates are marked in pen or rubber stamped. Tag is displayed in same location as regular plates on rear of vehicle. Dealers can issue a permit which is displayed in rear window.

permit

TEMP PASS CONN **690E0** Exp   Mo.   Day.   Yr.

DRIVER LICENSE

POLICE PATCH

Motorcycle

www.state.ct.us/dot
website

Special Plates

Environment

Greenway

College

Early American

NY Press

School Bus

Amistad

Animal Lover

DELAWARE

Passenger Plates and Renewal Decals

Front	Rear	YEAR EXPIRE	
		2002	**2003**
	THE FIRST STATE **123456** DELAWARE · MO YR	Decal Color Changes Monthly	Decal Color Changes Monthly

"The First State" issues one fully-reflectorized license plate for all vehicles. Delaware's plates are unique because they are neither embossed or debossed. They are made with silk-screening process and are completely flat . Passenger vehicle plates are all numeric.

Passenger Plates

Passenger regular

Personalized

Porcelain

Optional Graphic

Truck and trailer plate

Truck

Trailer

Apportioned Truck

Apportioned Trailer

Temporary Permit

DMV issues temporary cardboard permits validated by pen. "6 x 12") they are placed in the normal license plate position on the vehicle.

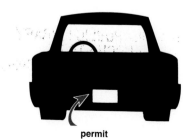

permit

DRIVER LICENSE

POLICE PATCH

Motorcycle

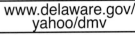

www.delaware.gov/
yahoo/dmv
website

Special Plates

Animal Friendly

Support Wildlife

Judge

Senator

Lions Club

Retired Military

Sorority

Private and Commercial

Delaware Devision of motor Vehicles.
P.O.Box 698, Dover, DE 19903   Tel. 302-739-4421

DC

Passenger Plates and Renewal Decals

Front	Rear	YEAR EXPIRE
		2002	2003

"The Capital City" issues two reflectorized plates to passenger vehicles. The new plate includes a political statement "taxatation without representation" to publisicize inability of DC resedents to vote in national elections.

Passenger Plates

| Passenger regular | Older issue | Disabled | Disabled Vet |

Truck and Trailer plate

| Truck | Trailer | Apportioned Truck |

Temporary Permit

DMV issues a paper permit (8¹/₂ x 5 ¹/₂") validated by marking pen. It has a sercurity hologram.

permit

26

POLICE PATCH

http://dc.gov/
website

DRIVER LICENSE

Special Plates

Innugural

Bicentennial

City Concil

Clergy

Taxi

Antique Car

U.S. Government

FLORIDA
Passenger Plates and Renewal Decals

Front	Rear	YEAR EXPIRE

2002 — 02 FL 05868108
2003 — 03 FL 05868108

"**The Sunshine state**" issues one fully-reflectorized license plate. All regular passenger plates display the county name (unless county officials request that "Sunshine State" be embossed instead). Florida has demonstrated that special licenses plates can be an excellent fund raising source raising millions to: save the Manatee, Florida Panther and memorialize the Challenger, as well as to promote other causes.

Passenger Plates

Passenger regular | Older issue | Older Issue | Personalized

Personalized | State owned | Highway Patrol

Truck and trailer plate

Truck | Permanent Trailer | Apportioned Truck 2002 Expire | Apportioned Truck 2003 Expire

Temporary Permit

Temporary 6" x 11" paper permits are issues by dealer, DMV or State tax agents. Validated by a marking pen t h e y are displayed inside the rear window or license plate position.

PLACED ON REAR WINDOW OR BUMPER

DRIVER LICENSE

POLICE PATCH

Motorcycle

FL

www.hsmv.state.fl.us/
website

Special Plates

Florida A&M

Gators

Barry University

Florida International

Wildlife

Everglades

Fishing

Save Manatee

Tampa Bay

Save Panther

Save Dolphins

Choose Life

Agriculture

Boy Scouts

Challenger New

Veterans

Support Education

Special Olympics

Medal Of Honor

State of the Arts

Florida Department of Highway Safety & Motor Vehicles
Neil Kirkman Building, 2900 Apalachee Parkway, Tallahassee, FL 32399
Tel. 904-922-9000

GEORGIA

Passenger Plates and Renewal Decals

Front	Rear	YEAR EXPIRE
		2002 2003

"The Peach State" issues one fully-reflectorized license plate with a uniform format and color scheme for each vehicle. Passenger plates display county name on a decal.

Passenger Plates

Passenger regular

Personalized

Disabled

Sheriff

Truck and trailer plate

Truck

Permanent Trailer

Private Truck
Apportioned

For Hire Truck
Apportioned 02 Expire

Temporary Permit

Temporary permits (paper) are issued only by county tag agents and must be displayed in rear window of passenger vehicles.

permit

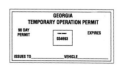

DRIVER LICENSE

POLICE PATCH

GA

www.dmvs.ga.gov/

website

Motorcycle

Special Plates

Spelman

Morris Brown college

Life College

Bulldogs

Georgia Southern

Wild Flower

Quail

Sons of Confederacy

Shriners

Purple Heart

Medal of Honor

National Guard

Korean War

Former POW

Pearl Harbor Survivor

Alternative Fuel

WW II Vet

Retired Vet

Korean War Vet

Desert Storm Vet

HAWAII

Passenger Plates and Renewal Decals

Front

HAWAII
HAA 123
ALOHA STATE

Rear

HAWAII MO/YR
HAA 123
ALOHA STATE

YEAR EXPIRE

2002
MAY
2002 A 000000

2003
MAY
2003 A 000000

The **"Aloha State"** issues two Fully-reflectorized license plates.

Passenger Plates

HAWAII
HAA 123
ALOHA STATE

Passenger regular

HAWAII
APPY
ALOHA STATE

Personalized

HAWAII
93
ALOHA STATE

Disabled

HAWAII MO/YR
D-2345-A
ALOHA STATE

Dealer Demo

Truck and trailer plate

HAWAII MO-YR
123 TBC
ALOHA STATE

Truck

HAWAII MO-YR
P1 2345
ALOHA STATE

Fleet

HAWAII MO-YR
012 WGN
ALOHA STATE

Horse and Wagon Plate

Temporary Permit

Dealers issue new vehicles a cardboard 30 day temporary plate (6" x 12") validated by pen.

permit

HAWAII

TEMPORARY LICENSE

DRIVER LICENSE

POLICE PATCH

Motorcycle

HI

www.hawaii.gov/dot/
website

Special Plates

Purple Heart

Combat Veteran

Electric Vehicle

Former Pow

Korea Veteran

Organization Plate

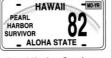

Pearl Harbor Survivor

Veteran

Vietnam Vet

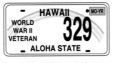

World War II Vet

Old Car

State Owned

IDAHO
Passenger Plates and Renewal Decals

Front	Rear	YEAR EXPIRE

2002 | **2003**

The **"Gem State"** home of "famous Potatoes" issues two fully-reflectorized license plates with a unique county code system. Counties are coded alphabetically; the tenth county starting with "B" received a "10B" prefix.

Passenger Plates

Passenger regular   Personalized   Disabled   State Police

Truck and trailer plate

Truck Apportioned   Truck   Apportioned Tractor

Temporary Permit

DMV issues a paper 30 days temporary registration validated by pen (8 x 4). It is displayed on rear window.

Special Plates

College   Kids   Sawtooth   Elk

34   Ski Mobile   Agriculture   Legislator   National Guard

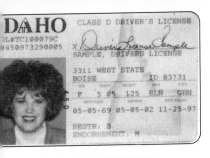

POLICE PATCH

ID

www.state.id.us/itd/dmv

website

DRIVER LICENSE

Motorcycle

Special Plates

Former POW

Purple Heart

Marine Veteran

Fire Fighter

Lewis & Clark

Wildlife

Collector Plate

Collector

Passenger vehicles and light trucks are issued plates with an alpha/numeric prefix which indicates the county of origin

The county (county seat) codes are as follows:

1A	Ada (Boise)	6C	Clearwater (Orofino)	N	Nez Perce (Lewiston)
2A	Adams (Council)	7C	Custer (Challis)	10	Oneida (Malad City)
1B	Bannock (Pocatello)	E	Elmore (Mtn. Home)	20	Owyhee (Murphy)
2B	Bear Lake (Paris)	1F	Franklin (Preston)	1P	Payette (Payette)
3B	Benewah (StMaries)	2F	Fremont (St. Anthony)	2P	Power (American Falls)
4B	Bingham (Blackfoot)	1G	Gem (Emmett)	S	Shoshone (Wallace)
5B	Blaine (Hailey)	2G	Gooding (Gooding)	1T	Teton (Driggs)
6B	Boise (Idaho City)	I	Idaho (Grangeville)	2T	Twin Falls (Twin Falls)
7B	Bonner (Sandpoint)	1J	Jefferson (Rigby)	V	Valley (Cascade)
8B	Bonneville (Idaho Falls)	2J	Jerome (Jerome)	W	Washington (Weiser)
9B	Boundary (Bonners Ferry)	K	Kootenai (Coeur d'Alene)		
10B	Butte (Arco)	1L	Latah (Moscow)		
1C	Camas (Fairfield)	2L	Lemhi (Salmon)		
2C	Canyon (Caldwell)	3L	Lewis (Nez Perce)		
3C	Caribou (Soda Springs)	4L	Lincoln (Shoshone)		
4C	Cassia (Burley)	1M	Madison (Rexburg)		
5C	Clark (Dubois)	2M	Minidoka (Rupert)		

Idaho Transportation department, Motor Vehicle Division
3311 West State Street, P.O. Box 7129, Boise, ID 83707-1129 Tel. 208-334-8000

ILLINOIS

Passenger Plates and Renewal Decals

Front	Rear	YEAR EXPIRE 2002	2003

The **"Land of Lincoln"** is issuing new plates to all 8.5 million vehicles. Beginning in 2001 a new Lincoln head design will be issued to passenger vehicles. This plate replacement program will be completed by 2003.

Passenger Plates

Passenger regular

Older issue

Personalize

New Personalized

Disabled

State Police

Sheriff

Truck and trailer plate

Truck

Truck Tractor

Trailer

Apportioned Truck

Temporary Permit

Temporary paper permits valid 60 days are issued by Sec. of state, and placed on windshield.

permit

36

DRIVER LICENSE

POLICE PATCH

Motorcycle

www.sos.state.il.us

website

Special Plates

Environment

Governer

Attorney General

Sec. of State

Disabled Veteran

Purple Heart

Pearl Harbor Survivor

Medal of Honor

FORMER POW

National Guard

Senate President

House

Consular

Foreign Org.

Speaker

Illinois Secretary of State's Office, Vehicle Service Department
Room 312, Howlett Building, 501 South Second Street, Springfield, IL 62756
Tel. 217-785-3000

INDIANA

Passenger Plates and Renewal Decals

Front	Rear	YEAR EXPIRE	
		2002	2003

Indiana "The Cross Road of America" issues one fully-reflectorized plate to passenger vehicles. A county code is included in the numbering prefix.

Passenger Plates

Passenger regular	Personalized	City Owned	State Official

Truck and trailer plate

Truck	Semi-Trailer	Apportioned Truck	Apportioned Trailer

Temporary Permit

Dealers issue a 31 day paper permit (8.5 x 5.5"). Validated by marking pen. It has a security strip down the middle.

Special Plates

Environment	Kids	Education	Boy Scouts
Health	Indians	Purple Heart	Arts
University	Lions	Shriner	4-H

38

DRIVER LICENSE

INDIANA STATE POLICE

POLICE PATCH

INDIANA
96050
MOTORCYCLE
Motorcycle

www.in.gov/bmv/
website

Special Plates

Food Bank

Girl Scouts

MASON

Pearl Harbor Survivor

Passenger vehicles and light trucks have a numeric prefixx that is a county code

The county and (county seats) are as follows:

1. Adams (Decatur)
2. Allen (Ft. Wayne)
3. Bartholomew (Columbus)
4. Benton (Fowler)
5. Blackford (Hrtfrd Cty.)
6. Boone (Lebanon)
7. Brown (Nashville)
8. Carroll (Delphi)
9. Cass (Logansport)
10. Clark (Jeffersonville)
11. Clay (Brazil)
12. Clinton (Frankfort)
13. Crawford (English)
14. Daviess (Washngtn.)
15. Dearborn (Lwrncbrg)
16. Decatur (Grensbrg.)
17. Dekalb (Auburn)
18. Delaware (Muncie)
19. Dubois (Jasper)
20. Elkhart (Goshen)
21. Fayette (Connersville)
22. Floyd (New Albany)
23. Fountain (Covington)
24. Franklin (Brookville)

25. Fulton (Rochester)
26. Gibson (Princeton)
27. Grant (Marion)
28. Greene (Bloomfield)
29. Hamilton (Nobles-ville)
30. Hancock (Greenfld.)
31. Harrison (Corydon)
32. Hendricks (Dansville)
33. Henry (New Castle)
34. Howard (Kokomo)
35. Huntingto (Hntgtn.)
36. Jackson (Brwnstwn.)
37. Jasper (Rnsselaer.)
38. Jay (Portland)
39. Jefferson (Madison)
40. Jennings (Vernon)
41. Johnson (Franklin)
42. Knox (Vincennes)
43. Kosciusko (Warsaw)
44. Lagrange (Lagrange)
45. Lake (Crown Point)
46. La Porte (La Porte)
47. Lawrence (Bedford)
48. Madiso (Anderson)

49. Marion (Indianapolis)
50. Marshall (Plymouth)
51. Martin (Shoals)
52. Miami (Peru)
53. Monroe (Bloomngtn.)
54. Montgomery (Crawfordsville)
55. Morgan (Martinsville)
56. Newton (Kentland)
57. Noble (Albion)
58. Ohio (Rising Sun)
59. Orange (Paoli)
60. Owen (Spencer)
61. Parke (Rockville)
62. Perry (Cannelton)
63. Pike (Petersburg)
64. Porter (Valpariso)
65. Posey (Mt Vernon)
66. Pulaski (Winamac)
67. Putnam (Greencstle.)
68. Randolph (Winchstr.)
69. Ripley (Versailles)
70. Rush (Rushville)
71. St.Joseph (S. Bend)
72. Scott (Scottsburg)
73. Shelby (Shelbyville)
74. Spencer (Rockport)
75. Starke (Knox)
76. Steuben (Angola)

77. Sullivan (Sullivan)
78. Switzerland (Vevay)
79. Tippecanoe (Lafayette)
80. Tipton (Tipton)
81. Union (Liberty)
82. Vanderburgh (Evansville)
83. Vermillion (Newport)
84. Vigo (Terre Haute)
85. Wabash (Wabash)
86. Warren (Williamsport)
87. Warrick (Boonville)
88. Washington (Salem)
89. Wayne (Richmond)
90. Wells (Bluffton)
91. White (Monticello)
92. Whitley (Colmb.Cty.)
93. Marion (Indianapolis)
94. Lake (Crown Point)
95A. Military & Special
95B -Z. Marion (Indianapolis)
96. Lake (Crown Point)
97-99 Marion (Indianapolis)

IOWA

Passenger Plates and Renewal Decals

Front	Rear	YEAR EXPIRE	
		2002	2003

The **"Hawkeye State"** issues two Fully-reflectorized plates. The County name appears on the bottom of passenger and truck plates.

Passenger Plates

Passenger regular

Personalized

Disabled

Dealer

Truck and trailer plate

Truck

Apportioned Trailer

Apportioned Power Unit

Apportioned Truck

Temporary Permit

DOT and Authorized dealers issue 30 day temporary permits (paper), Validated by marking pen.

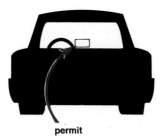

permit

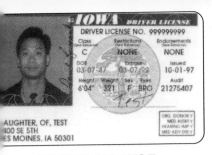

DRIVER LICENSE

AUGHTER, OF, TEST
400 SE 5TH
ES MOINES, IA 50301

POLICE PATCH

www.dot.state.ia.us/

website

Motorcycle

Special Plates

Collegiate
Hawkeyes

Collegiate
Cyclones

Panthers

State Owned

Disabled

Disabled Vet

National Guard

Medal of Honor

Purple Heart

State Police

Environmental

Cattlemen Care

Fire Fighter

Veteran

Pearl Harbor Vet

EX- POW

wa Department of Transportation, Motor Vehicle Division
0 Euclid Avenue, P.O. Box 9278, Des Moines, IA 50306-9278   Tel. 515-237-3110

KANSAS

Passenger Plates and Renewal Decals

Front	Rear	YEAR EXPIRE
		2002 2003

The" **Sunflower State**" issues one fully-reflectorized license plate each
containing a small two-letter county designation decal in an upper corner
of the plate. Personalizes plates are issued in pairs, and are a different graphic design

Passenger regular

Older issue valid 02

Personalize

Disabled

Truck and trailer plate

Apportioned Truck

Apportioned Trailer

Truck intra-state

Trailer intra-state

Temporary Permit

permit

Special Plates

Purple Heart

National guard

Former POW

Pearl Harbor survivor

Kansas State

KU

State Owned

Dealer

POLICE PATCH

Motorcycle

KS

DRIVER LICENSE

County Sticker Codes

Kansas uses a 2 alpha county code on passenger plates. It appears on a decal on the upper left corner of the plate. The counties and (county seats) are as follows:

AL ALLEN (Iola)
AN ANDERSON (Garnett)
AT ATCHISON (Atchison)
AB BARBER (Medicine Lodge)
BT BARTON (Great Bend)
BB BOURBON (Ft. Scott)
BR BROWN (Hiawatha)
BU BUTLER (El Dorado)
CS CHASE (Ctnwood Falls)
CQ CHAUTAUQUA (Sedan)
CK CHEROKEE (Columbus)
CN CHEYENNE (St Francis)
CA CLARK (Ashland)
CY CLAY (Clay Center)
CD CLOUD (Concordia)
CF COFFEY (Burlington)
CM COMANCHE (Coldwtr.)
CL COWLEY (Winfield)
CR CRAWFORD (Girard)
DC DECATUR (Oberlin)
DK DICKINSON Abilene)
DP DONIPHAN(Troy)
DG DOUGLAS (Lawrence)
ED EDWARDS (Kinsley)
EK ELK (Howard)
EL ELLIS (Hays)
EW ELLSWORTH (Ellswrth)
FI FINNEY (Garden City)
FO FORD (Dodge City)
FR FRANKLIN (Ottawa)
GE GEARY (Junction City)
CO GOVE (Gove)
GH GRAHAM (Hill City)
GT GRANT (Ulysses)
GY GRAY (Cimarron)
GL GREELEY (Tribune)

GW GREENWOOD (Eureka)
HM HAMILTON (Syracuse)
HP HARPER (Anthony)
HV HARVEY (Newton)
HS HASKELL (Sublette)
HG HODGEMAN (Jetmore)
JA JACKSON (Holton)
JF JEFFERSON(Oskaloosa)
JW JEWELL (Mankato)
JO JOHNSON (Olathe)
KE KEARNY (Lakin)
KM KINGMAN (Kingman)
KW KIOWA (Greensburg)
LB LABETTE (Oswego)
LE LANE (Dighton)
LV LEAVENWORTH (Leavenworth)
LC LINCOLN (Lincoln)
LN LINN (Mound City)
LG LOGAN (Oakley)
LY LYON (Emporia)
MN MARION (Marion)
MS MARSHALL (Marysville)
MP McPHERSON (McPherson)
ME MEADE (Meade)
MI MIAMI (Paola)
MC MITCHELL (Beloit)
MG MONTGOMERY (Independence)
MR MORRIS (Council Grove)
MT MORTON (Elkhart)
NM NEMAHA (Seneca)
NO NEOSHO (Erie)
NS NESS (Ness City)
NT NORTON (Norton)
OS OSAGE (Lyndon)
OB OSBORNE (Osborne)

OT OTTAWA(Minneapolis)
PN PAWNEE (Larned)
PL PHILLIPS (Phillipsburg)
PT POTTAWATOMIE (Westmoreland)
PR PRATT (Pratt)
RA RAWLINS (Atwood)
RN RENO (Hutchinson)
RP REPUBLIC (Belleville)
RC RICE (Lyons)
RL RILEY (Manhattan)
RO ROOKS (Stockton)
RH RUSH (La Crosse)
RS RUSSELL (Russell)
SA SALINE (Salina)
SC SCOTT (Scott City)
SG SEDGWICK (Wichita)
SW SEWARD (Liberal)
SN SHAWNEE (Topeka)
SD SHERIDAN (Hoxie)
SH SHERMAN (Goodland)
SM SMITH (Smith Center)
SF STAFFORD (St John)
ST STANTON (Johnson)
SV STEVENS (Hugoton)
SU SUMNER (Wellington)
TH THOMAS (Colby)
TR TREGO (Wakeeney)
WB WABAUNSEE (Alma)
WA WALLACE (Sharon Springs)
WS WASHINGTON (Washington)
WH WICHITA (Leoti)
WL WILSON (Fredonia)
WO WOODSON (Yates Center)
WY WYANDOTTE (Kansas City)

nsas **Department of Revenue, Division of Motor Vehicles**
bert B. **Docking Office Blvd. First Floor, Topeka, KS 66626-0001** Tel.913-296-3601

KENTUCKY

Passenger Plates and Renewal Decals

Front	Rear	YEAR EXPIRE 2002	2003

The **"Bluegrass State"** issues one fully -recflectorized graphic license plate for all passenger vehicles. A county name decal appears at the bottom of the plate.

Passenger Plates

Passenger regular

Personalized

Disabled

City/County Owned

Truck and trailer plate

Truck Limited Use

Truck Apportioned

Trailer

Truck

Temporary Permit

Licensed dealers and county agents issue a cardboard permit (51/2 x 11") validated by marking pen. Valid up to 30 days it has a security hologram.

permit

Special Plates

Cardinal

National Guard

Bird Cenus

College

Purple Heart

Care about Kids

Horse

Mason

44

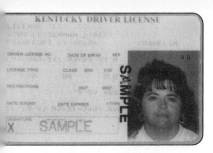

DRIVER LICENSE

POLICE PATCH

Motorcycle

www.kytc.state.ky.us/
website

Special Plates

Farm

Military Reserve

Retired Veteran

Korean Veteran

Gulf War Veteran

WW II Veteran

Disabled Vet

College

LOUISIANA

Passenger Plates and Renewal Decals

Front   **Rear**   **YEAR EXPIRE**

2002   2003

The **"Sportman's Paradise"** issues one 3 alpha - 3 numeric fully-reflectorized passenger license plate to passenger vehicle.

Passenger Plates

| Passenger regular | Personalized | Disabled | Disabled Vet |

Truck and trailer plate

| Comm. Truck | Private Truck | Private Truck | Apportioned |

Temporary Permit

Dealers, auto title Company and lending instutions issues a 60 day paper permit (6 x 12") validated by pen.

permit

Special Plates

C.A.P   Save Bear   Bobwhite   Safe Kids

E.M.S   Grambling Univ.   Former POW   Pearl Harbor Survivor

46

DRIVER LICENSE

POLICE PATCH

www.dps.state.la.us/
dpsweb.nsf
website

Motorcycle

Special Plates

Educator

Vol. Fire Fighter

Hearing Impaired

Veteran

Agriculture

Ducks Unlimited

College

Wild Turkey

Lions Club

Louisiana Department of Public Safety, Vehicle Registration Bureau
P.O. Box 64886, Baton Rouge, LA 70896   Tel. 504-925-6335

MAINE

Passenger Plates and Renewal Decals

Front	Rear	YEAR EXPIRE 2002	2003

MAINE 02 0627718

MAINE 03 0627718

"America Vacationland" issues two fully-reflectorized license plates.

MAINE 12345 - MUNICIPAL -

MAINE 123-456 - STATE -

Passenger regular	Personalized	City Owned	State Owned

Truck and trailer plates

MAINE EXP•2•29•04 123456 - APPORTIONED -

MAINE 123456 COMMERCIAL

Semi- Permanent Trailer	Apportioned Truck	Apportioned Trailer	Commercial Truck

Temporary Permit

Motor Vehicle Bureau issues 12 x6" cardboard temp. validated by marking pen. Valid 60 days.

Also a cardboard Transit plate is valid for 1 trip within a 15 day period. it cannot be renewed.

MAINE-TEMP

Issued____Month____Day, Expires____Month____Day

MAINE-TRANSIT 115-718
Issued____Month____Day, Expires____Month____Day

permit   permit

Temporary plates are displayed either inside the rear window or the normal plate posi

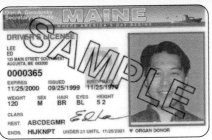

DRIVER LICENSE

POLICE PATCH

Motorcycle

www.state.me.us/sos/

website

Special Plates

Indian Representative

Senate

House

Medal Of Honor

Disabled Veteran

Combat Wounded

Pearl Harbor Survivor

Former POW

Veteran

Environment

University Of Maine

Sheriff

Maine Secretary of State's Office, Bureau of Motor Vehicles
29 State house station, Augusta, ME 04333   Tel. 207-287-8637

49

MARYLAND

Passenger Plates and Renewal Decals

Front	Rear	YEAR EXPIRE	
		2002	2003

The **"Old Line State"** issues two fully-reflectorized license plates. Passenger and many other non-passenger types display the colorful state shield.

Passenger Plates

Passenger regular	Personalized	Disabled	Local Govt.

Truck Apportioned	Truck/Trailer

Temporary Permit

Authorized Maryland auto dealers can issue a 45 day cardboard tag, validated by pen. sie (6 x 12")

MVA provides cardboard 15 day permit for Maryland new owners to drive to an inspection facility. size (6 x 12")

permit

DRIVER LICENSE

POLICE PATCH

Motorcycle

www.mdot.state.md.us

website

Special Plates

Environment

State owned

National Guard

Bowling

Farm

Firemen

Amateur Radio

Veteran

Port Towns

Pets

Scuba Diver

Dental Health

MASSACHUSETTS

Passenger Plates and Renewal Decals

Front	Rear	YEAR EXPIRE
		2002 2003

The **"Bay State"** issues two fully-reflectorized graphic license plate
Earlier issued green on white plate are still in use.

Passenger Plates

Passenger regular	Older issue valid 02	Personalized	Reserved Series Low Numbers

Truck and trailer plates

Apportioned Truck	Comm. Truck	Apportioned Truck 2002 Expire

Temporary Permit

Massachusetts does not issue any type of temporary permi
to operate a passenger vehicle.

DRIVER LICENSE

POLICE PATCH

Motorcycle

Special Plates

Cape Code

Amateur Radio

Save the Whale

Trout

Industrial Heritage

Veteran

Senate

State Police

Invest in Kids

Private School Bus

Dealer

City Owned

MICHIGAN

Passenger Plates and Renewal Decals

Front	Rear	YEAR EXPIRE	
		2002	2003

The **"Great Lakes State"** issues one partially-reflectorized (glass beads on paint background) white on blue license plate. Personalized plates are issues in pairs.

Passenger Plates

Passenger regular · Personalized · Disabled · Sheriff

Truck and trailer plates

Truck GVW · Apportioned Truck · 5 Year Trailer · Apportioned Trailer

Temporary Permit

Secretary of State and branch offices issue a
14 -60 day paper permit (5 x8")

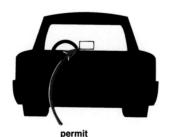

permit

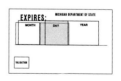

DRIVER LICENSE

POLICE PATCH

Motorcycle

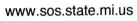

www.sos.state.mi.us

website

Special Plates

Optional Graphic Bridge

Auto Commemorative

Agriculture

Light House

Protect Water

Children

Vietnam Vet

Wildlife

Ferris State

Grand Valley Univ.

Tech University

Northern University

Oakland University

Saginaw University

Michigan Univ.

Michigan Univ. Flint

Medal of Honor

Purple Heart

Firemen

Lions

Michagan Department of State, Motor Vehicle Administration
7064 Crowner Drive, Lansing, MI 48918 Tel. 517-322-6331

55

MINNESOTA

Passenger Plates and Renewal Decals

Front	Rear	YEAR EXPIRE	
		2002	**2003**

The **"Land of 10,000 Lakes"** issues two fully-reflectorized license plates. Most non-passenger vehicle plates are non-graphic.

Passenger Plates

Passenger regular	Older issue	Personalize	Disabled

Truck and trailer plates

Truck Commercial Zone	Apportioned	Commercial Truck	Truck Farm

Temporary Permit

Minnesota auto dealers can issue a 21 day temporary registration when permanent plates are not available. This paper document must be affixed to the inside of the rear window.

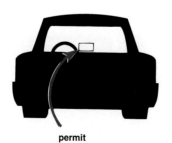

permit

POLICE PATCH

Motorcycle

www.dot.state.mn.us/
website

DRIVER LICENSE

Special Plates

Environment

Laos Veteran

Purple Heart

Pearl Harbor Survivor

Collegiate

Restricted Use

Tax Exempt

State Owned

Dealer

Morris College

St. John's Univ.

Gustavus College

innesota Department of Public Safety, Driver and Vehicles Div.
3 Transportation Bldg. 395 John Ireland Blvd., St Paul, MN 55155 Tel. 612-296-2001

MISSISSIPPI

Passenger Plates and Renewal Decals

Front	Rear	YEAR EXPIRE
		2002 2003

The **"Magnolia State"** issues one fully-reflectorized license plate. The county name is appeared on bottom of a plate.

Passenger Plates

Passenger regular   Personalized   Disabled   Highway Patrol

Truck and trailer plates

Apportioned   Truck   Semi-Trailer   Farm

Temporary Permit

Mississippi does not use temporary plates or permit to newly purchased passenger vehicles. The owner has a seven working days grace period to obtain plates from the county tax office.

DRIVER LICENSE

POLICE PATCH

www.state.ms.us/
website

Motorcycle

Special Plates

Jackson State Univ.

MISSISSIPPI
10R69
Ole Miss

MSU
Ole Miss

State Univ.

Wildlife

MISSISSIPPI
102 W Y
Conserving Wildlife

Turkey

Wildlife

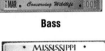

Bass

Trout

Deer

MISSISSIPPI
2909 W Y
Conserving Wildlife

Butterfly

Fire Fighter

Retired Military

Veteran

Choose Life

MISSOURI

Passenger Plates and Renewal Decals

Front	Rear	YEAR EXPIRE 2002	2003

The **"Show-Me State"** issues two fully-reflectorized license plates
On passenger vehicles.

Passenger Plates

Passenger regular	Personalized	Disabled	Highway Patrol

Truck and trailer plates

Truck Local	Truck Beyond Local	Apportioned Truck	Permanent Trailer

Temporary Permit

**Dealers can issue paper temporary 20 day
permit validated by marking peb. It is displayed
on the rear window of the vehicle**

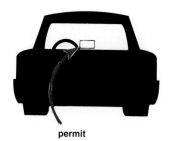

permit

MISSOURI
DRIVER LICENSE
License Number 222222222
SAMPLE
JANE
0 ANY STREET
JEFFERSON CITY MO 65101
Birthdate 10-14-1963
Expiration Date 10-14-2004
Female 5'06 110 lbs Blue Eyes
Restrictions Endorsements
Class F

DRIVER LICENSE

POLICE PATCH

642-BZ

Motorcycle

www.modot.state.mo.us/
website

Special Plates

Medal Of Honor

MISSOURI •JUL
CONGRESSIONAL
MEDAL OF HONOR

MISSOURI
5001PW
MO FORMER P O W 98

Former POW

MISSOURI
500 1NG
MO NATIONAL GUARD 98

National Guard

MISSOURI
DVO 123
MO DISABLED VETERAN 98

Disabled Vet

D V 3 123
MO DISABLED VETERAN 98

Disabled Veteran

MISSOURI
100 1NR
MO NAVY RESERVE 98

Navy Reserve

MISSOURI •JUL
12 0PH
PURPLE HEART

Purple Heart

MISSOURI
123 0RN
MO RETIRED MILITARY 98

Retired Military

OCT MO
12345
SAINT LOUIS UNIVERSITY

St. Louis Univ.

OCT MO
OZARK
COLLEGE OF THE OZARKS

College of Ozarks

JAN MO
12345

MSU

MISSOURI
FSRI
MO FIRE FIGHTER 98

Fireman

MISSOURI
CH 001
JUN CONSERVATION 02

Conservation

MISSOURI
CH 002
JUN CONSERVATION 02

Conservation

MISSOURI
CH 003
JUN 02

Conservation

MISSOURI
D874-E
DEC DEALER

Dealer

MISSOURI
CTF

Children Trust Fund

MISSOURI
MGL
MO FREEMASON 98

Freemason

Missouri Department of Revenue, Divison of Motor Vehicles
Harry S. Truman State Office Building
P.O.Box 100, Jefferson City MO 65105   Tel. 573-751-4429

MONTANA
Passenger Plates and Renewal Decals

Front	Rear	YEAR EXPIRE	
		2002	2003

The **"Big Sky Country"** issues two Fully-reflectorized license plates. The numeric prefix indicates county of origin. The letter P is no longer included in the county prefix.

Passenger Plates

Passenger regular	Older issue	Personalized	Disabled

State owned

Truck and trailer plates

Truck	Trailer	Trailer	Apportioned

Temporary Permit

County Treasures issue a letter size computer typed 20 or 60 day permit. This sheet is displayed on window. Dealers usa a printed form (8 x 6) Valid 20 days.

 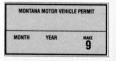

Special Plates

Rocky Mountain Col.	Northern Montana col.	Univ. of Montana	Collector

National Guard	Marine Vet	Amateur Radio	Disabled

POLICE PATCH

Motorcycle

www.doj.state.mt.us/mvd

website

DRIVER LICENSE

---

first 1 or 2 numbers characters on passenger truck and large trailer plates is a county code.
county code (County Seats are as follows:

The first 1 or 2 numeric characters on passenger, truck and large trailer plates is a county code; The county code (county seats) are :

1 - Silver Bow (Butte)
2 - Cascade (Great Falls)
3 - Yellowstone (Billings)
4 - Missoula (Missoula)
5 - Lewis & Clark (Helena)
6 - Gallatin (Bozeman)
7 - Flathead (Kalispell)
8 - Fergus (Lewistown)
9 - Powder River (Broadus)
10 - Carbon (Red Lodge)
11 - Phillips - (Malta)
12 - Hill (Havre)
13 - Ravalli (Hamilton)
14 - Custer (Miles City)
15 - Lake (Polson)
16 - Dawson (Glendive)
17 - Roosevelt (Wolf Point)
18 - Beaverhead (Dillon)
19 - Chouteau (Ft. Benton)
20 - Valley (Glasgow)
21 - Toole (Shelby)
22 - Big Horn (Hardin)
23 - Musselshell (Roundup)
24 - Blaine (Chinook)
25 - Madison (Virginia City)

26 - Pondera (Conrad)
27 - Richland (Sidney)
28 - Powell (Deer Lodge)
29 - Rosebud (Forsyth)
30 - Deer Lodge (Anaconda)
31 - Teton (Chouteau)
32 - Stillwater (Columbus)
33 - Treasure (Hysham)
34 - Sheridan (Plentywood)
35 - Sanders (ThompsonFalls)
36 - Judith Basin (Stanford)
37 - Daniels (Scobey)
38 - Glacier (Cut Bank)
39 - Fallon -(Baker)
40 - Sweet Grass (Big Timber)
41 - McCone (Circle)
42 - Carter (Ekalaka)
43 - Broadwater (Townsend)
44 - Wheatland (Harlowton)
45 - Prairie (Terry)
46 - Granite (Philipsburg)
47 - Meagher (Whte Sul Spgs)
48 - Liberty (Chester)

49 - Park (Livingston)
50 - Garfield (Jordan)
51 - Jefferson (Boulder)
52 - Wibaux (Wibaux)
53 - Golden Valley (Ryegate)
54 - Mineral (Superior)
55 - Petroleum (Winnett)
56 - Lincoln (Libby)

NEBRASKA

Passenger Plates and Renewal Decals

Front	Rear	YEAR EXPIRE	
		2002	**2003**

The **"Cornhusker State"** issues two fully-reflectorized license plate. A new Sandhill Crane design was introduced Jan 2001. Three numeric- three alpha designator is used for Douglas, Lancaster, Serpy counties a county name sticker attached to the bottom of the plate. All other counties use the 1- through 93 prefix code.

Passenger Plates

Passenger regular (Omaha)

Passenger regular (Hooker)

Older Issue

Disabled

Truck and trailer plates

Truck Commercial	Apportioned Power Unit	Apportioned Trailer	Trucks used for water and soil conservation

Temporary Permit

Licensed dealers can issue Nebraska residents a paper IN TRANSIT permit validated by pen and displayed in the rear window (6 x 8 ")

30 day standard size metal plates are issued to non-resident car buyers to drive their car home.

permit

Special Plates

Amateur Radio

Husker Fan

Husker Fan 02

Purple Heart

POLICE PATCH

Motorcycle

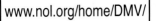

www.nol.org/home/DMV/

website

DRIVER LICENSE

Nebraska passenger vehicle license plates have a numeric county prefix followed by an alpha and numerics.

The county prefixes and (county seats) are as follows:

1 - Douglas (Omaha)
2 - Lancaster (Lincoln)
3 - Gage (Beatrice)
4 - Custer (Broken Bow)
5 - Dodge (Fremont)
6 - Saunders (Wahoo)
7 - Madison (Madison)
8 - Hall (Grand Island)
9 - Buffalo (Kearney)
10 - Platte (Columbus)
11 - Otoe (Nebraska City)
12 - Knox (Center)
13 - Cedar (Hartington)
14 - Adams (Hastings)
15 - Lincoln (North Platte)
16 - Seward (Seward)
17 - York (York)
18 - Dawson (Lexington)
19 - Richardson (Falls City)
20 - Cass (Plattsmouth)
21 - Scotts Bluff (Gering)
22 - Saline (Wilber)
23 - Boone (Albion)
24 - Cuming (West Point)
25 - Butler (David City)
26 - Antelope (Neligh)
27 - Wayne (Wayne)
28 - Hamilton (Aurora)
29 - Washington (Blair)
30 - Clay (Clay Center)
31 - Burt (Tekamah)
32 - Thayer (Hebron)
33 - Jefferson (Fairbury)
34 - Fillmore (Geneva)
35 - Dixon (Ponca)
36 - Holt (O'Neill)
37 - Phelps (Holdrege)
38 - Furnas (Beaver City)

39 - Cheyenne (Sidney)
40 - Pierce (Pierce)
41 - Polk (Osceola)
42 - Nuckolls (Nelson)
43 - Colfax (Schuyler)
44 - Nemaha (Auburn)
45 - Webster (Red Cloud)
46 - Merrick (Central City)
47 - Valley (Ord)
48 - Red Willow (McCook)
49 - Howard (St. Paul)
50 - Franklin (Franklin)
51 - Harlan (Alma)
52 - Kearney (Minden)
53 - Stanton (Stanton)
54 - Pawnee (Pawnee City)
55 - Thurston (Pender)
56 - Sherman (Loup City)
57 - Johnson (Tecumseh)
58 - Nance (Fullerton)
59 - Sarpy (Papillion)
60 - Frontier (Stockville)
61 - Sheridan (Rushville)
62 - Greeley (Greeley)
63 - Boyd (Butte)
64 - Morrill (Bridgeport)
65 - Box Butte (Alliance)
66 - Cherry (Valentine)
67 - Hitchcock (Trenton)
68 - Keith (Ogallala)
69 - Dawes (Chadron)
70 - Dakota (Dakota City)
71 - Kimball (Kimball)
72 - Chase (Imperial)
73 - Gosper (Elwood)
74 - Perkins (Grant)
75 - Brown (Ainsworth)
76 - Dundy (Benkelman)

77 - Garden (Oshkosh)
78 - Deuel (Chappell)
79 - Hayes (Hayes Center)
80 - Sioux (Harrison)
81 - Rock - (Bassett)
82 - Keya Paha (Springview)
83 - Garfield (Burwell)
84 - Wheeler (Bartlett)
85 - Banner (Harrisburg)
86 - Blaine (Brewster)
87 - Logan (Stapleton)
88 - Loup (Taylor)
89 - Thomas (Thedford)
90 - McPherson (Tryon)
91 - Arthur (Arthur)
92 - Grant (Hyannis)
93 - Hooker (Mullen)

All Nebraska registered trucks carry a tonnage sticker on their license plate.

Nebraska Department of Motor Vehicles, Rigistraton and Titles Division.
301 Centennial Mall South, P.O. Box 94789, Lincoln NE 68509-4789   Tel. 402-471-3918

NEVADA

Passenger Plates and Renewal Decals

Front	Rear	YEAR EXPIRE	
		2002	2003

The **"Silver State"** issues two fully-reflectorized license plates.
Many older plate designs are still in use.

Passenger Plates

Passenger regular	Optional Graphic	Older Issue	Older Issue

Centennial	Disabled	State Owned

Truck and trailer plates

Apportioned	Truck	Trailer Apportioned	Semi - Trailer

Temporary Permit

Nevada dealers issue a 10 day special paper permit to
new car owner which is displayed on the lower right hand
corner of the windshield. Size is 5" x 4".

permit

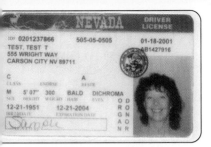

DRIVER LICENSE

POLICE PATCH

Motorcycle

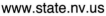

NV

www.state.nv.us

website

Special Plates

Marine Vet

Lake Tahoe

Agriculture

Personalized

Kids Art

Purple Heart

Air Force Vet

Navy Vet

NEW HAMPSHIRE

Passenger Plates and Renewal Decals

Front	Rear	YEAR EXPIRE	
		2002	2003

The **"Granite State"** issues two fully-reflectorized license plates with the unique slogan Live Free or Die".

Passenger Plates

Passenger regular

Older issue

Personalized

Personalized

Disabled

Dealer

Truck and trailer plates

Apportioned

Commercial Truck

Farm

Trailer

Temporary Permit

Dealers issue a red and white temporary permit (6 x 12") valid 20 days.

NEW HAMPSHIRE TEMP.
315141
MONTH   DAY

Dealers issue a brown and white temporary permit (6 x 12") valid 20 days

NEW HAMPSHIRE TEMP.
076496
MONTH   DAY

permit

DRIVER LICENSE

POLICE PATCH

website

Motorcycle

Conservation

Dealer

National Guard

Veteran

Antique

NEW JERSEY

Passenger Plates and Renewal Decals

Front	Rear	YEAR EXPIRE	
		2002	**2003**

The **"Garden State"** issues Two Fully-reflectorized license plates. In 1999 they began using validation stickers on the plates replacing the windshield stickers formerly used.

Passenger Plates

Passenger regular	Older issue	Courtesy plate	Disabled

Truck and trailer plates

Apportioned	Truck	Trailer

Temporary Permit

Licensed dealers and DMV officers issue 20 day paper permit (6 x 14) validated by ink marker

permit

Special Plates

Medal of Honor	Battle Ship	Marine	Baymen

Animal Friendly	Wildlife	Jersey Shore	Wildlife

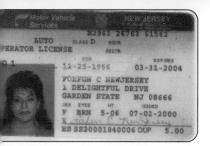

DRIVER LICENSE

POLICE PATCH

Motorcycle

pecial Plates

Pinelands

Olympic

EMT

Fire Fighter

First Aid

Hospital

Liberty Island

Trees

Meadowlands

NEW MEXICO
Passenger Plates and Renewal Decals

Front	Rear	YEAR EXPIRE 2002	2003

The **"Land of Enchantment"** issues one fully-reflectorized license plate a county name appears at the top of most plate and the zia Indian Sun -sign separates the numbers from letters. And optional graphic balloon plate is also available

Passenger Plates

Passenger regular	Optional Graphic	Personalized	Personalized

Truck and trailer plates

Truck	Apportioned	Trailer

Temporary Permit

New and used car dealers, and motor vehicle field officers can issue an 30 day paper permit (81/2" x 51/2") validated by marking pen.

permit

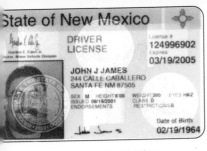

DRIVER LICENSE

POLICE PATCH

P06522

Motorcycle

www.state.nm.us/state/htd.html

website

Special Plates

G 29996
Government
New Mexico USA

Government

US 1517
LAND OF ENCHANTMENT
NEW MEXICO MO/YR

Indian Tribal Vehicle

Veteran

State Senator

MP 215
MOUNTED PATROL
New Mexico USA

Mounted Patrol

National Guard

Purple Heart

Navy Veteran

NW5D
MOUNTED PATROL
New Mexico USA

Amateur Radio

Disabled Vet

Fire Fighter

Fire Fighter

KID 0000
Children's Trust Fund
New Mexico USA

Kids Trust

Marine Vet

Medal of Honor

NM Univ.

New Mexico Taxation & Revenue Department, Motor Vehicle Division
P.O. Box 1028, Santa Fe, NM 87594   Tel. 505-827-2294

73

NEW YORK

Passenger Plates and Renewal Decals

Front	Rear	YEAR EXPIRE	
		2002	**2003**

Windshield Decals   Windshield Decals

The **"Empire State "** issues two fully-reflectorized license plates.
A windshield decal is use for validation New York offers over
300 custom (special) plates for an extra fee.

Passenger Plates

Passenger regular	Older issue	Personalized	Disabled

Truck and trailer plates

Commercial Truck	Truck Older Issue	Apportioned	Apportioned Trailer

Temporary Permit

DMV or Dealers issue a paper (12 x 5") in
transit permit validated by marking pen.
Permits are attached to the rear window

permit

Special Plates

College and University Plates

Notre Dane	Dowling College	Fordham Univ.	West Point

Regional Plates

74 Adirondacks	Manhattan	Niagara County	Nassau County

DRIVER LICENSE

POLICE PATCH

Motorcycle

www.nydmv.state.ny.us

website

Special Plates

Military Plates

Purple Heart

Vietnam Vet

Infantry Combat Badge

WW II Vet

Special Cause Plates

State of the Arts

Pets

Harley Owner

Horse Racing

Professional

Acupuncturist

CPA

EMT

Medical Doctor

Sports Plates

Jets

Knicks

Mets

Rangers

Sports Plates

Number One

NASCAR®

Earnhart

Parks

NORTH CAROLINA

Passenger Plates and Renewal Decals

Front	Rear	YEAR EXPIRE	
		2002	2003

The **"Tarhill State"** issues one fully-reflectorized License plate. The last general issue was in 1980 so there are many older plates in use (some are not reflectorized).

Passenger Plates

MO First in Flight YR	MO First in Flight YR	MO First in Flight YR	N.C. PERMANENT
GZA-1234	OAKLEY	♿HD1234	PX1234
NORTH CAROLINA	NORTH CAROLINA	NORTH CAROLINA	
Passenger regular	Personalized	Disabled	State owned

Truck and trailer plates

N.C. PERMANENT	TRAILER	NORTH CAROLINA	N.C. COMMERCIAL 02
LD-1101	AR-85592	AY-16400	LZ-8700
APPORTIONED	NORTH CAROLINA	MULTI-YEAR	APPORTIONED
Truck Apportioned	Trailer	Trailer Multi-Year	Apportioned Annual

Temporary Permit

A(6 x 12") multi-use cardboard tag is issued by dealers and DMV as a temporary permit. Validated by marking pen it is attached to the rear of the car.

MULTI USE TAG
NORTH CAROLINA
TN-50575
ISSUED MAKE IDENTIFACTION EXPIRES

permit

Special Plates

UNC	NC State	Appalachian	Clemson

Duke	East Carolina	UNC Wilmington	Univ. South Carolina

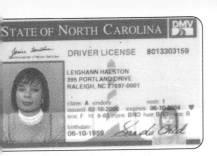

DRIVER LICENSE

POLICE PATCH

www.dmv.dot.state.nc.us
website

Motorcycle

Special Plates

Pearl Harbor survivor

Naval Reserve

Purple Heart

American Legion

Legion of Valor

Silver Star

Bronze Star

Disabled Vet

DFC

Army Reserve

Civil Air Patrol

Retired Coast Guard

Hatteras Lighthouse

Wildlife

Fire and Rescue

Friends of Smoky Mountain

NORTH DAKOTA

Passenger Plates and Renewal Decals

Front	Rear	YEAR EXPIRE 2002	2003

The **"Peace Garden State"** issues two fully-reflectorized license plates.

Passenger regular

Disabled

State owned

Truck and trailer plates

Apportioned Power Unit

Trailer

Apportioned

Temporary Permit

Auto dealers issue paper DRIVE OUT PERMITS (4X4")
which are attached inside the glass of a vehicle to be
registered out-of-state.
A copy ot the LICENSE APPLICATION (81/2 x 3")
is displayed on vehicles to be registered in
North Dakota

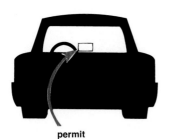

permit

 DRIVE OUT PERMIT (4 X 4)

NOTARY OR DEALER LICENS
APPLICATION (81/2 X 3)

DRIVER LICENSE

POLICE PATCH

Motorcycle

www.state.nd.us/dot/
website

Special Plates

Commemorative

Chippewa
(issued by tribe)

Chippewa
(issued by tribe)

Spirit Lake
(issued by tribe)

Former POW

Disabled Vet

Amateur Radio

Marine Vet

**North Dakota department of Transportation, Motor Vehicle Division.
608 East Boulevard Ave., Bismarck ND 58505-0780   Tel. 701-328-2725**

OHIO

Passenger Plates and Renewal Decals

Front	Rear	YEAR EXPIRE	
		2002	2003

The **"Buckeye State"** issues two fully-reflectorized license plates. A new bicentennial design was introduced October 1, 2001 the county name decal has been replaced by a county code decal. All county are numbered in alphabetical order 1 -88 (1- ADAMS, 88 - WYANDOTTE)

Passenger regular   Older issue   Older issue   Personalized

Apportioned   Truck   Trailer

Temporary Permit

Dealers can issue a cardboard temporary tag (6x12")
for use while title is process to reflect the name of the new owner.

permit   permit   Q737599

Special Plates

Maimi Univ.   Ohio State Univ.   Bowling Green Univ.   College

Cleveland State Univ.   Univ. of Dayton   Dennison Univ.   Kent State Univ.

DRIVER LICENSE

POLICE PATCH

www.dot.state.oh.us/
website

Motorcycle

Special Plates

Kids

National Guard

Disabled Vet

Court ordered

Environment

Wildlife

Organization

Eagle Scout

Disabled

DU

Future Farmers

Scenic Rivers

Football

Boy Scouts

Cleveland Browns

Wildlife

Ohio Bureau of Motor Vehicles
4300 Kimberly Parkway, PO Box 16520 Colombus, OH 43266-0020
Tel 614-752-7100 1800-589-TAGS

OKLAHOMA
Passenger Plates and Renewal Decals

Front	Rear	YEAR EXPIRE	
		2002	2003

The **"Sooner State"** issues one fully-reflectorized license plate. Several older designs are still in use.

Passenger Plates

Passenger regular

AD-1234

Older issue

Older issue

Older issue

HD-123

Disabled

DOKEY

Personalized
Available in 6 Colors

Truck and trailer plates

476-OAA

Trailer

1HP 901

Apportioned

THN-522

Truck older Issue

TAB 138

Commercial Truck

Temporary Permit

Each Auto Dealer issues a temporary notice of there own design which is displayed on the rear window the new car owner can obtain regular plates

ASHA MOTORS

permit

Special Plates

Wildlife

Wildlife

ENV 123

Environment

HRT 123

Heartland

IWO 245

IWO JIMA Vet

123 SPR

Olympic Spirit

066 RTE

Route 66

123 HST

Native Heritage

82

DRIVER LICENSE

POLICE PATCH

Motorcycle

www.oktax.state.ok.us

website

Special Plates

Connors State

East OK State Col.

OK STATE

Univ. of OK

Rogers State Col.

Rose State Col.

S.E. OK State

S.W. OK State

D-Day Survivor

Military Decorations

Military Decorations

Gold Star

Korea Vet

National Guard

WW II Vet

EX-POW

Oklahoma Tax Commission Motor Vehicle Division
2501 N. Lincoln Boulevard, Oklahoma City. OK 73194   **Tel. 405-521-2510** 83

OREGON
Passenger Plates and Renewal Decals

Front	Rear	YEAR EXPIRE	
		2002	2003

The **"Pacific Wonderland"** issues two fully-reflectorized license plates.
Several older plates designs are still in use.

Passenger Plates

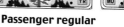

Passenger regular	Older issue	Older issue	Personalized

Truck and trailer plates

Apportioned Truck	Commercial Truck	Permanent Trailer	Apportioned Light Tru•

Temporary Permit

**Dealers and DMV officers issues paper trip permits
(7" x 41/2") validated by pen permit is displayed
rear window.**

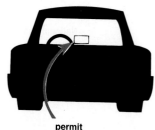

permit

Special Plates

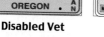

Salmon	Disabled Vet	Elected Official	National Guard

DRIVER LICENSE

POLICE PATCH

Motorcycle

www.odot.state.or.us

website

Special Plates

Disabled Vet

Purple Heart

Korean Vet

First Marine Division

Veteran

Amateur Radio

Antique

Special Interest

OSU Ducks

Oregon State Beavers

Western Oregon Univ.

PENNSYLVANIA

Passenger Plates and Renewal Decals

Front	Rear	YEAR EXPIRE
		2002 2003

MO/YR **PENNSYLVANIA**
ABC·1234
— WWW.STATE.PA.US —

PENNSYLVANIA
1-02
0000211

PENNSYLVANIA
1-03
0000211

The **"Keystone State"** Issue one fully-reflectorized license plate. It is the first state to include the web address in the design.

Passenger Plates

PENNSYLVANIA
ABC·1234
— WWW.STATE.PA.US —

Passenger regular

KEYSTONE STATE
BAA·1234
MO/YR PENNSYLVANIA

Older issue

KEYSTONE STATE
NED
MO/YR PENNSYLVANIA

Personalized

PENNSYLVANIA
ESTHER
— WWW.STATE.PA.US —

Personalized Current Design

PENNSYLVANIA
♿ 2149A
— WWW.STATE.PA.US —

Disabled

PENNSYLVANIA
HE-03022
— HEARING IMPAIRED —

Hearing Impaired

PENNSYLVANIA
H10-836H
— DEALER —

Dealer

Truck and trailer plates

PENNSYLVANIA
YDL-6774
— TRUCK —

Truck

PENNSYLVANIA
BN-00123
— APPORTIONED —

Apportioned Truck

PENNSYLVANIA
XM-31546
— TRAILER —

Trailer

Temporary Permit

Dealers and authorized agents
can issue a cardboard plate(6 x 12")
to vehicles to be registered in another state.
This plate is validated by pen and a hole punch.

PENNSYLVANIA
3120-796
30 DAY TEMPORARY TRANSIT
EXPIRATION DATE PUNCHED IN BORDER

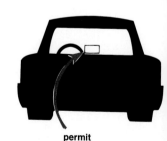

permit

Special Plates

D
A 123 D.A.R.E.
PENNSYLVANIA

86   **D.A.R.E.**

COMBAT WOUNDED VETERAN
PH 12 30
MO/YR PENNSYLVANIA

Purple Heart

• DISABLED VETERAN •
DV-12345
PENNSYLVANIA

Disabled Veteran

PENNSYLVANIA
SAM CMH
MEDAL OF HONOR

Medal of Honor

DRIVER LICENSE

POLICE PATCH

Motorcycle

Special Plates

PA. Zoo

PA Railroad

Wildlife

Wildlife

Penn. State Alummi

DU

Fire Fighter

Amateur Radio

School Vehicle

Barbershop

Steel Worker

National Guard

Marine Corps League

Marine Reserve

VFW

Notre Dame

**Pennsylvania Department of transportation. Bureau of Motor Vehicles
River Front Office Center, #rd Floor, 1101 South Front St.
Harrisburg, PA 17104-2516   Tel. 717-783-6517**

RHODE ISLAND

Passenger Plates and Renewal Decals

Front	Rear	YEAR EXPIRE

		2002 2003

The **"Ocean State"** issues two fully-reflectorized license plates. Plates are revalidated for a two year period.

Passenger Plates

Passenger regular	Personalized	Optional Graphic	State Owned

Truck and trailer plates

Truck Commercial	Trailer	Apportioned Truck

Temporary Permit

20 day cardboard dealer permits are red and white and validated by dealer number and expire stamped in black.

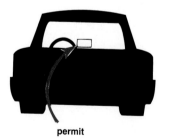

permit

```
STATE OF RHODE ISLAND
20 DAY TEMPORARY PLATE
71309-K
DEALER NO.   EXPIRES ON
   MONTH   DAY  YEAR
```

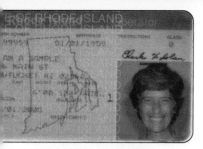

DRIVER LICENSE

POLICE PATCH

Motorcycle

Special Plates

Jitney

Antique Vehicle

Veteran

Purple Heart

SOUTH CAROLINA

Passenger Plates and Renewal Decals

Front **Rear**

Smiling Faces. Beautiful Places.
123 ABC
South Carolina

YEAR EXPIRE

2002
SC **02**
0000000

2003
SC **03**
0000000

The **"Palmetto State"** issues one fully-reflectorized license plate.

Passenger Plates

Smiling Faces. Beautiful Places.
123 ABC
South Carolina

Nothing Could Be Finer
GOPHER
South Carolina

D. VETERAN
V 1234
South Carolina

Passenger regular   **Personalized**   **Disabled Vet**

Truck and trailer plates

20 • SOUTH CAROLINA • 01
P100001
TRUCK

• SOUTH CAROLINA •
TL10001
TRAILER

• SOUTH CAROLINA •
P70000
APPORTIONED

Truck   **Trailer**   **Apportioned**

Temporary Permit

DMV and authorized dealers issue 20 day temporary cardboard plates validated by ink marker.

20 DAY PLATE
SOUTH CAROLINA
TP-092001
ISSUED   MAKE   IDENTIFICATION   EXPIRES

permit

Special Plates

• Clemson •
T1990
South Carolina

The University of
U1993
South Carolina

ANDERSON COLLEGE
AC1998
South Carolina

Bob Jones University
J1993
South Carolina

Clemson   **Univ. of SC**   **Anderson College**   **Bob Jones Univ.**

College of Charleston
CH1
South Carolina

THE CITADEL
B1993
South Carolina

CLAFLIN
CP1
South Carolina

COLUMBIA COLLEGE
CL1
South Carolina

Charleston Col.   **The Citadel**   **Claflin Col.**   **Columbia Col.**

90

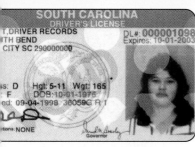

DRIVER LICENSE

POLICE PATCH

Motorcycle

www.dot.state.sc.us
website

Converse Col.

Charleston Southern Univ.

Erskine Col.

ST. Francis Col.

Furman

Lander Univ.

Limestone Col.

Morris Col.

Newberry Col.

North Greenville Col.

Presbyterian Col.

Southern Wesleyan Univ.

Education

EMT

Fire Fighter

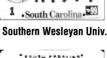

Amateur Radio

Wildlife

Environment

Pearl Harbor Survivor

Purple Heart

Highway Comm.

Military Reserve

Shirner

Shag

S.C Department of Revenue, Division of Motor Vehicles
P.O.Box 1498, Columbia, SC 29216- 0008   Tel. 803-737-1153   91

SOUTH DAKOTA
Passenger Plates and Renewal Decals

Front	Rear	YEAR EXPIRE	
		2002	2003

The **"Home Of Mount Rushmore"** issues two fully-reflectorized license plates. The prefix on each passenger plate is a county code.

Passenger Plates

| Passenger regular | Personalized | Disabled | City Owned |

Truck and trailer plates

| Commercial Truck | Apportioned | Apportioned Trailer Permanent |

Temporary Permit

Temporary permit are issued to passenger cars by county treasurer high patrol or DMV. These green paper forms are attached to the lower left corner of the windshield.

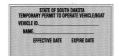

permit

Special Plates

| Organization Plate | Disabled Vet | Fire Fighter | Tuskegee Univ. |

| Medal of Honor | Pearl Harbor Survivor | Crow Creek Sioux | Lower Brule Sioux |

| 92 Rosebud Sioux | Standing Rock Sioux | Sisseton Wahpeton Sioux | Yankton Sioux |

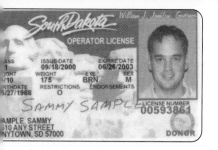

DRIVER LICENSE

POLICE PATCH

Motorcycle

Special Plates

The first two characters on a plate is a county code
The code and county (county seats) are as follows:

1	Minnehaha (Sioux Falls)	27	Fall River (Hot Springs)	52	Moody (Flandreau)
2	Pennington (Rapid City)	28	Faulk (Faulkton)	53	Perkins (Bison)
3	Brown (Aberdeen)	29	Grant (Milbank)	54	Potter (Gettysburg)
4	Beadle (Huron)	30	Gregory (Burke)	55	Roberts (Sisseton)
5	Codington (Watertown)	31	Haakon (Philip)	56	Sanborn (Woonsocket)
6	Brookings (Brookings)	32	Hamlin (Hayti)	57	Spink (Redfield)
7	Yankton (Yankton)	33	Hand (Miller)	58	Stanley (Fort Pierre)
8	Davison (Mitchell)	34	Hanson (Alexandria)	59	Sully (Onida)
9	Lawrence (Deadwood)	35	Harding (Buffalo)	60	Tripp (Winner)
10	Aurora (Plankinton)	36	Hughes (Pierre)	61	Turner (Parker)
11	Bennett (Martin)	37	Hutchinson (Olivet)	62	Union (Elk Point)
12	Bon Homme (Tyndall)	38	Hyde (Highmore)	63	Walworth (Selby)
13	Brule (Chamberlain)	39	Jackson (Kadoka)	64	Ziebach (Dupree)
14	Buffalo (Gannvalley)	40	Jerauld (Wessington Sprgs.)	65	Shannon (*Wounded Knee)
15	Butte (Belle Fourche)	41	Jones (Murdo)	66	Yankton (Yankton)
16	Campbell (Mound City)	44	Kingsbury (De Smet)	67	Todd (Mission)
17	Charles Mix (Lake Andes)	43	Lake (Madison)	65,67	Are entirely within native American reservations
18	Clark (Clark)	44	Lincoln (Canton)	77	Dealer plate
19	Clay (Vermillion)	45	Lyman (Kennebec)		
20	Corson (McIntosh)	46	McCook (Salem)		
21	Custer (Custer)	47	McPherson (Leola)		
22	Day (Webster)	48	Marshall (Britton)		
23	Deuel (Clear Lake)	49	Meade (Sturgis)		
24	Dewey (Timber Lake)	50	Mellette (White River)		
25	Douglas (Armour)	51	Miner (Howard)		
26	Edmunds (Ipswich)				

Commercial vehicles are issued multi-year plates. The characters are 1 alpha -4 numeric and the year and ton weight class appears on the validation decal.

South Dakota tax-exempt plates are issued to state, city, county and tribal-owned vehicles.

The following alpha prefix codes are used:

CO - County-owned
CY - City-owned
GFP - Game, Fish, Park Dept.

HP - Highway Patrol
SC, ED - School vehicles
DE - Driver's education

South Dakota Department of Revenue, Divison of Motor Vehicles
118 West Capitol Avenue, Pierre, SD 57501-2080
Tel. 605-773-3545

TENNESSEE

Passenger Plates and Renewal Decals

Front	Rear	YEAR EXPIRE	
		2002	2003

The **"Volunteer State"** issues one fully-reflectorized license plate. The County origin appears on a decal at the bottom of each passenger plate. Many counties impose a wheel tax and require a decal on the plate.

Passenger Plates

Passenger regular   **Personalized**   **Disabled**   **State Owned**

Truck and trailer plates

Semi-Trailer   **Apportioned**   **Truck**

Temporary Permit

Cardboard Permit (5 x 7) are issue by county clerk highway patrol and Dept. of Safety. Validated by pen there are displayed on rear window

permit

Special Plates

Agriculture   **State Park**   **Smokey Mtns.**   **Tenn.Walking horse**

Animal Friendly   **Wildlife**   **Wildlife**   **Square Dance**

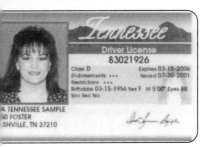

DRIVER LICENSE

POLICE PATCH

www.state.tn.us
website

TN

Motorcycle

Special Plates

State Senate

WW II Veteran

Korean War Vet

Veteran

UT

Sewanee

Tenn. State

Arkansas Univ.

Univ. of Florida

Univ. of Tenn.

Martin

Enemy Evader

Amateur Radio

Children First

Cool Cat

DU

Fire Fighter

Lions Club

MADD

Mason

Wildlife

Lake Radnor

Silly Fish

Sportsman

Tennessee Department of Revenue, Motor Vehicle Commission
Titiling & registration Divison, 44 Vantage Way, Suite 160
Nashville, TN 37243   Tel 615-4   -6851

95

TEXAS

Passenger Plates and Renewal Decals

Front	Rear	YEAR EXPIRE
		**2002** **2003**
		WINDSHIELD STICKER **WINDSHIELD STICKER**

The **"Lone Star State"** issues two fully-reflectorized license plates.
A windshield decal is used for vehicle validation.

Passenger Plates

Passenger regular   Passenger older edition 1998   Passenger older edition 1990   Passenger older edition

Truck and trailer plates

Truck   Truck Apportioned   Trailer

Temporary Permit

Automobile dealers print their own temporary paper permits which they give to new car buyers. Validated by marking pen they are placed on the rear window or normal plate location.

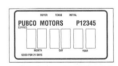

permit

permit

Special Plates

Colleges and University

Southwest Texas Univ.

McMurray Univ.

Texas A&M Univ.

Rice Univ.

Baylor Univ.

Sam Houston State

Huston Tillotson

SMU Univ.

96

DRIVER LICENSE

POLICE PATCH

Motorcycle

www.dot.state.tx.us

website

TX

pecial Plates

National guard

Purple Heart

U.S. Air Force

Armed Forces Res.

U.S. Army

Civil Air Patrol

Disabled Vet

Marine Corps

U.S. Navy

Vietnam Vet

WW II Vet

Ham Radio

Animal Friendly

Bigbend Park

Parks and Wildlife

Peace Officer

Reading

Grapefruit

State of the Arts

Ducks Unlimited

Texas Department of Transportation, Vehicle Titles and Registration Division
4000 Jackson Avenue, Austin TX 78779-0001   Tel. 512-302-2076

UTAH

Passenger Plates and Renewal Decals

Front

Rear

YEAR EXPIRE

2002

2003

The **"Beehive State"** issues two fully-reflectorized license plates. A county decal (with two alpha design) is displayed on the upper left hand corner of the rear plate.

Passenger Plates

Passenger regular

Passenger regular

Personalized

Personalized

Disabled

Truck and trailer plates

Truck Apportioned

Truck Apportioned

Truck

Trailer

Temporary Permit

30 day temporary paper permits (10 x 4') are issue by dealers and DMV. There can be placed anywhere on the vehicle where it is visible no less than 30 feet.

Special Plates

Colleges and University

Brigham Young Univ.

Westminster College

Wildlife

Highway Patrol

98 **Manufacturer**

Olympic

Pearl Harbor Survivor

Collector

POLICE PATCH

www.sr.ex.state.ut.us

website

Motorcycle

DRIVER LICENSE

Special Plates

National Guard

Honors Veteran

Invest in Kids

Snowmobile

Wildlife

Wildlife

County of origin appears on a 2 alpha decal applied to the upper left corner of the plate.

The counties and (county seats) are as follows:

BV - Beaver (Beaver)
BE - Box Elder (Brigham City)
CA - Cache (Logan)
CC - Carbon (Price)
DG - Daggett (Manila)
DA - Davis (Farmington)
DU - Duchesne (Duchesne)
EM - Emery (Castle Dale)
GA - Garfield (Panguitch)
GR - Grand (Moab)
RN - Iron (Parowan)
JU - Juab (Nephi)
KA - Kane (Kanab)
MD - Millard (Fillmore)

MN - Morgan (Morgan)
PT - Piute (Junction)
RH - Rich (Randolph)
SL - Salt Lake (Salt Lake City)
SJ - San Juan (Monticello)
SP - Sanpete (Manti)
SE - Sevier (Richfield)
SU - Summit (Coalville)
TE - Tooele (Tooele)
UN - Uintah (Vernal)
UT - Utah (Provo)
WA - Wasatch (Heber City)
WN - Washington (St. George)

WE - Wayne (Loa)
WB - Weber (Ogden)

VERMONT

Front	Rear	YEAR EXPIRE 2002	2003

The " **Green Mountain**" issues two fully-reflectorized license plates.

Passenger Plates

Passenger regular	Personalized	Disabled

Truck and trailer plates

Truck	Trailer	Interstate Truck Special Weight	Apportioned Truck

**Vermont uses temporary plates (6 x 12")
DMV tags are black on white dealers tag
are red on white.**

permit

DRIVER LICENSE

POLICE PATCH

Motorcycle

Special Plates

Fireman

Environment

Amateur Radio

Sheriff

Purple Heart

National Guard

Pearl Harbor Survivor

Municipal Owned

Vermont Agency of Transportation, Department of Motor Vehicles
120 State Street, Montpelier, VT 05603-0001   Tel. 802-828-2020

VIRGINIA

Passenger Plates and Renewal Decals

Front	Rear	YEAR EXPIRE	
		2002	**2003**

Front
MO · Virginia · YR
ZYZ-4132

Rear
MO · Virginia · YR
ZYZ-4132

EXPIRES LAST DAY OF
JAN 0 2
0002751

EXPIRES LAST DAY OF
JAN 0 3
0002751

The **"Old Dominion State"** issues two fully-reflectorized plates.
Virginia coined the term communiplate to promote the sales of
special plates which has generated 20,000,000 Dollars of new revenue.

Passenger Plates

· Virginia · **ZYZ-4132**	MO · VIRGINIA · YR **RBC - 123**	MO · Virginia · YR **BONNIE**	· VIRGINIA · **31-249S** · OFFICIAL STATE USE ONLY ·
Passenger regular	Older issue	Personalized	State Owned

Truck and trailer plates

VA APPORTIONED **123456 P** PERMANENT	VA TRACTOR H **13579** X A PERMANENT	VIRGINIA **102030** T R PERMANENT TRAILER	VA TRUCK H **77077** H A PERMANENT
Apportioned Truck	Tractor	Trailer	Truck

Temporary Permit

Dealers issue temporary cardboard plates(6 x 12")
red on white validated by marking pen.

THIRTY DAY TAG
ISSUE ☐ EXPIRES ☐
MAKE ☐ SERIAL ☐
V I R G I N I A
Z979-462

permit

Special Plates

Colleges and University

MO · VIRGINIA · YR **UV1234** ·UNIVERSITY of VIRGINIA·	· VIRGINIA · **ONE** · RUTGERS UNIVERSITY ·	· VIRGINIA · **ND 51** · UNIVERSITY OF NOTRE DAME ·	JUL · VIRGINIA · 01 **UR1719** · UNIVERSITY OF RICHMOND ·
The University	Rutgers	Notre Dame	Richmond Univ.

Special Plates

BEA-UTY VIRGINIA	MO · VIRGINIA · YR **123●456**	MO ♫VIRGINIA YR **PIPER**	MONTH VIRGINIA YEAR **BONNIE** 1607 JAMESTOWN
Virginia Heritage	Great Seal	Patriot	Jamestown

POLICE PATCH

www.dmv.state.va.us
website

970375

Motorcycle

DRIVER LICENSE

Special Plates

C12345

easure The Chesapeake

VIRGINIA GREAT2C

Scenic

1234BA

Wildlife

7717

George Washington

G. Washington

LV1001
LIONS OF VIRGINIA

Lions Club

VIRGINIA SUNFUN
VIRGINIA BEACH

Virginia Beach

VIRGINIA DILLON

Wildlife

VIRGINIA 1414AX
ALEXANDRIA • 1999

Alexandra

HEATHER

Autumn Leaves

VIRGINIA 1014BD
WILDLIFE CONSERVATIONIST

Wildlife

VIRGINIA CHRISAN
DRIVE SMART

Buckle Up

VIRGINIA 1605EG
WILDLIFE CONSERVATIONIST

Wildlife

VIRGINIA BOBS
National Air and Space Museum
DULLES CENTER

Dulles Center

VIRGINIA 138 4ES
EASTERN SHORE

Eastern Shore

VIRGINIA ♥1347HT

Family

VIRGINIA 1354GA
SUPPORTER OF GREYHOUND ADOPTION

Greyhound Rescue

VIRGINIA ALPCA
KEEP THE LIGHTS SHINING

Lighthouse

VIRGINIA 3340BF
TIGER SWALLOWTAIL
STATE INSECT

Wildlife

VIRGINIA 191●6NR

N.R.A.

VIRGINIA 1211MW
M.W. PRINCE HALL G.L.

Prince Hall

Commonwealth of Virginia, Department of Motor Vehicles.
2300 West Board Street, P.O. Box 27412, Richmond, VA 23269-0001
Tel. 804-367-0538

WASHINGTON

Passenger Plates and Renewal Decals

Front	Rear	YEAR EXPIRE

Front

WASHINGTON MO YR
523-GYZ
EVERGREEN STATE

Rear

WASHINGTON MO YR
523-GYZ
EVERGREEN STATE

YEAR EXPIRE

2002
X 000000
2002
THE FUTURE IS NOW

2003
X 000000
2003
THE FUTURE IS NOW

The **"Evergreen State"** issues two fully-reflectorized license plates. Many older issue are still in use.

Passenger Plates

WASHINGTON MO YR
523-GYZ
EVERGREEN STATE

Passenger regular

ABC 123

Older issue

MO Washington YR
MARTHA

Personalized

MO WASHINGTON YR
ROSS

Personalized older issu

Truck and trailer plates

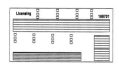

WASHINGTON MO YR
12345PR
APPORTIONED

Truck Apportioned

MO Washington YR
85632-L
Centennial Celebration

Truck

MO Washington YR
7890-JX
Centennial Celebration

Trailer

WASHINGTON MO/YR
BY1234

Truck Older Issue

Temporary Permit

Dealers issue a paper issue which is displayed on the rear window.

Licensing 189701

permit

Special Plates

Washington 98
04378
H U S K I E S
UW

Huskies

Washington
0000
WESTERN
WWU

West Washington Univ.

MO Washington YR
FORMER PRISONER OF WAR
123
Centennial Celebration

Former POW

MO Washington YR
PEARL HARBOR SURVIVOR
123
Centennial Celebration

Pearl Harbor Survivor

MO Washington YR
H L K
0010A
Centennial Celebration

Hulk Hauler

Washington
0000 DV

Disabled Veteran

Washington
NOABC

Amateur Radio

Washington
AFAOZZ

M.A.R.S.

POLICE PATCH

www.wsdot.wa.gov/
website

Motorcycle

DRIVER LICENSE

Special Plates

Purple Heart

Veteran

Stadium

Ride Share

Disabled Parking

Square Dance

Antique Car

Washington State Department of Licensing, Bureau of Motor Vehicles
P.O. Box 48001, Olympic WA, 98504-8001   Tel. 360-902-3600

WEST VIRGINIA

Passenger Plates and Renewal Decals

Front   **Rear**   **YEAR EXPIRE**
    2002   2003

The **"Mountain State"** issues one fully-reflectorized license plate to passenger vehicles.

Passenger Plates

Passenger regular

Optional Graphic

Personalized

Disabled

Truck and trailer plates

Apportioned Truck

Trailer 10 YRS

Apportioned Trailer Long Term

Truck

Temporary Permit

Dealers and DMV issue a paper 60 day permit which has a security strip. Validated by pen it is displayed on the rear window.

permit

Special Plates

Colleges and University

Marshall Univ.

WVU Mountaineers

Concord College

Weslyn College

Graphic

EMS

Police Assn.

Wildlife

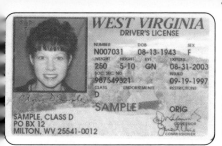

DRIVER LICENSE

POLICE PATCH

Motorcycle

www.state.wv.us/wvdot

website

Veteran

Senate

Post Master

House

National Guard

Purple Heart

Marine League

Pearl Harbor Survivor

Former POW

Disabled Vet

Medal of Honor

Fire Fighter

Elks

Amateur Radio

Mason

Professional Fireman

Shrine

Square Dance

Rotary

Bowler

NASCAR®

Rusty Wallace

Dale Earnhardt

Dale Earnhardt Jr

est Virginia department of Transportation, Division of Motor Vehicles
uilding 3, Kanawha Blvd, East, Charleston, WV 25317   Tel. 304-558-2723

WISCONSIN

Passenger Plates and Renewal Decals

Front	Rear	YEAR EXPIRE
WISCONSIN 234 ABD *America's Dairyland*	**WISCONSIN** 234 ABD MO *America's Dairyland* YR	2002 2003

"America's Dairyland" issue two fully-reflectorized license plates to passenger vehicles.

Passenger Plates

Passenger regular	Older issue	Personalized	Disabled

Truck and trailer plates

Truck Apportioned	Truck Multi-Year	Semi -Trailer	Truck Private Carrier

Temporary Permit

DMV and Dealers issue a cardboard temporary plate (6 x 12") validated by pen,

Special Plates

Colleges and University

Wisconsin Univ. (Standard Plate Design)	Wisconsin Univ. (Standard Plate Design)	Environmental	Sesquicentennial

Tribal	Celebrate Children	Amateur Radio	Repossessor

DRIVER LICENSE

POLICE PATCH

www.dot.state.wi.us
website

Motorcycle

ecial Plates

State Owned

County Owned

Ducks Unlimited

Korean Veteran

Antique Car

Collector

Hobbyist

Fire Fighter

National Guard

Disabled Veteran

Football Fan

onsin Department of Transportation Division of Motor Vehicles,
Sheboygan Avenue P.O. Box 7911, Madison, WI 53707-7911   Tel.608-266-2233

WYOMING

Passenger Plates and Renewal Decals

Front	Rear	YEAR EXPIRE	
		2002	2003

3 - 02 WYOMING 00355869

3 - 03 WYOMING 00355869

The **"Equality State"** issues two fully-reflectorized license plates to passenger. Wyoming has featured a bucking bronco on it's plates since 1936.

Passenger Plates

Passenger regular	Older issue	Personalized	City Owned

Truck and trailer plates

Apportioned Truck	Apportioned Trailer	Trailer	Truck

Temporary Permit

Dealers issue a 45 day cardboard temporary permit validated by pen. It has a security hologram strip.

permit

Special Plates

Air National Guard	Army National Guard	Disabled Veteran	Former POW

Pearl Harbor Survivor	Dealer Demo	State Owned	County Owned

POLICE PATCH

www.state.wy.us

website

Motorcycle

DRIVER LICENSE

All Wyoming private and commercial license plates are issued by county treasurers and they have a numeric prefix which identifies the issuing county.

Wyoming has 23 counties and the prefix code, county and (county seat) are:

Prefix	County	County seat
1	Natrona	Casper
2	Laramie	Cheyenne
3	Sheridan	Sheridan
4	Sweetwater	Rock Springs
5	Albany	Laramie
6	Carbon	Rawlins
7	Goshen	Torrington
8	Platte	Wheatland
9	Big Horn	Basin
10	Fremont	Lander
11	Park	Cody
12	Lincoln	Kemmerer

Prefix	County	County seat
13	Converse	Douglas
14	Niobrara	Lusk
15	Hot Springs	Thermopolis
16	Johnson	Buffalo
17	Campbell	Gillette
18	Crook	Sundance
19	Uinta	Evanston
20	Washakie	Worland
21	Weston	Newcastle
22	Teton	Jackson
23	Sublette	Pinedale
99	Rental fleet vehicle	

Amateur radio, apportioned and pioneer plates have no county code.
Air National Guard plates have all even numerics; Army Guard has odd numerics.

State and other government owned vehicle plates have
prefix codes. Multiple-character prefixes are stacked:

**Wyoming Department of Transportation, Licensing and Titling Section
P.O. Box 1708, Cheyenne, WY 82003-1708 Tel. 307-777-4709**

ALBERTA

1 PLATE VALIDATED
BY 2 DECALS
CAN BE RE-VALIDATED
FOR 2 YR PERIOD

DRIVER'S LICENSE

MOTORCYCLE

PASSENGER REGULAR
3 ALPHA - 3 NUMERIC
(CLASS 3)

PERSONALIZED
2 PLATES ISSUED

DISABLED - WHEELCHAIR
DECAL IS OPTIONAL
PLATE BEGINS WITH "A"

CLASS 1 PLATE
(PUBLIC SERVICE)

CLASS 2 PLATE, FARM
DECAL FOR PURPLE GAS

CLASS 4 PLATE

PLATE VALIDATION

MONTH   YEAR

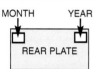

REAR PLATE

YEAR EXPIRE 02

YEAR EXPIRE 03

www.gov.ab.ca/

Alberta issues the same Wild Rose Country graphic design plate to all classes of vehicles. Whenever captions are used they appear on the upper right corner and are self-explanatory. Passenger car plates are 3 alpha - 3 numeric, and no codes are used.

Alberta has four regular classes and six special plates. The regular classes can be identified by a spacer dot •.

Class 1(Public Service vehicles) One numeric followed by a dot i.e. **1• 12345,** or 1 alpha and 5 numerics **B-01234.** Includes :Buses, livery, car rental, truck rental, public service trailer, driveaway

Class 2 2 numerics followed by dot , example. **46-A123.** Includes:Farm vehicle, nurseryman, Transport own goods,private. bus, Gen. merch. for hire.

Class 3 3 alpha dot 3 alpha i.e. **ABC•123.** Includes:Passenger, motorcycle, Govt, driveaway, transport own goods, commercial trailer.

Class 4 4 numerics dot 2 numerics i.e. **1234 • 56,** or 1 alpha, 3 numerics- 2 numerics: **A123-45** issued to :Trailers

Special plates are: Antique, Consular ,Dealer, Disabled, Ham radio. All are captioned

License plates are issued at random within a class, therefore it is not possible to distinguish between types. For example a rental car , a livery and a driveaway are all class 1 and have a single alpha or numeric prefix. Prefix VE6 is reserved for Ham radio operators. No other codes are used.

Alberta Registries
Motor Vehicle Division, Direct Customer Service
9th Floor, John E. Brownlee Bldg., 10365 97th St., Edmonton
Alberta, Canada T5J 3W7   Tel. 403-427-8250

BRITISH COLUMBIA

2 PLATES VALIDATED
BY 1 DECAL REAR PLATE

DRIVER'S LICENSE

MOTORCYCLE

PERSONALIZED

AMATEUR RADIO

FOREIGN CONSUL

COMMERCIAL TRUCK

APPORTIONED

ANTIQUE CAR

PLATE VALIDATION

FRONT PLATE

REAR PLATE

MO/YR

YEAR EXPIRE 02

YEAR EXPIRE 03

www.th.gov.bc.ca/tran/

* includes Yukon & N.W.T.

British Columbia issues 3 alpha - 3 numeric plates to passenger vehicles. There are no county of origin, weight or special use codes. The plate characters are for individual vehicle identification only.

Trucks, trailers and other commercial vehicle tags are 2 alpha - 4 numeric and these codes are used:

Prefix
A - Farm truck
D - Demonstrator
F - Farm tractor
MA- Auto-manufacturer
R - Repairer
P - Apportioned
TF - Trailer floater
TR - Transporter
X - Industrial equipment.

Suffix
2 alpha - Commercial truck
1 Numeric 1 Alpha - Commercial trailer
SA - Special agreement plate- for mining
equipment limited use of the highway.

The weight of a vehicle does not appear on a B.C.license plate.

Insurance Corporation of British Columbia (ICBC)
136 151 West Esplanade
North Vancouver, British Columbia V7M 3H9
Tel. 604-661-6348

MANITOBA

Passenger
2 plates

DRIVER'S LICENSE

MOTORCYCLE
DEALER

PASSENGER - 1983 ISSUE
2 PLATES

OFF ROAD

PERSONALIZED CAN
BE ON 1983 OR 1987 BASE

PUBLIC SERVICE TRUCK

LOCAL TRUCK
SUFFIX BEGINS WITH
LETTER T,Y,Z

COMMERCIAL TRUCK

PLATE VALIDATION

DAY   MO/YR

REAR PLATE

YEAR EXPIRE 02	YEAR EXPIRE 03

www.gov.mb.ca

Manitoba issued a new graphic design plate to all vehicles during 1998. 2 plates per vehicle are required. Most plates are 3 alpha-3 numeric and special class identification stickers are used on some commercial plates. List of reserved plate prefixes and sticker symbols are below.

alpha prefix		Sticker codes	
C	Commercial		
CAL	Commercial trailer	CL	Country livrey
CC	Consular Corps	DA	Drive away
D	Dealer	LM	Limousine
P	Public service	F	Farm truck
PAL	Public service truck	T	Truck
R	Repairer	TX	Taxi, livrey
VE4	Amateur radio(Ham)	SV	Snow vehicle
X	Taxi, livery		

Manitoba Highways & Transportation
Division of Driver & Vehicle Licensing, 1075 Portage Ave.
Winnipeg, Manitoba R3G 0S1

NEW BRUNSWICK

BAA-123

2 PLATES VALIDATED
BY 1 DECAL ON BOTH PLATES

DRIVER'S LICENSE

MC47600

MOTORCYCLE

123 456

conservation

AMP
AM1-151

AMPUTEE

ANTIQUE
AA1-234

ANTIQUE AUTO

1

LIEUTENANT GOVERNOR

CAA-123

LT. COMMERCIAL VEHICLE

VE1PJJ

AMATEUR RADIO

TAA-001

TRAILER

L50-001

LARGE COMMERCIAL VEHICLE

DP-301

DIPLOMAT

PLATE VALIDATION

MO/YR

FRONT PLATE

MO/YR

REAR PLATE

YEAR EXPIRE 02

0000000 N.B.
03/2002

YEAR EXPIRE 03

0000000 N.B.
03/2003

www.gov.nb.ca

New Brunswick issues 3 alpha - 3 numeric character plates to passenger cars, beginning at BAA-001. These plates were first issued May 1, 1991, and were used on all types of vehicles by april 1992. All types have uniform design.Light Commercial, truck ,tractor trailer and farm plates have a 1,2 or 3 alpha prefix code. .Special prefixes to look for on New Brunswick license plates:

AM - Amputee
D - Dealer
DP - Diplomat
CAA - CZZ - Lt. commercial vehicle
F - Farm truck
HA - Transporter
L - Large commercial vehicle
M - Miscellaneous

MC - Motorcycle
P - Farm produce transporter
PR - Pro rated vehicle
TA - Trailer
TAA - TZZ - Trailer
VE1 - Amateur Radio

New Brunswick Motor Vehicle Branch
P.O.Box 6000
Fredericton , N.B. E3B 5H1

NEWFOUNDLAND & LABRADOR

2 PLATES VALIDATED
BY 1 DECAL
ON REAR PLATE

DRIVER'S LICENSE

MOTORCYCLE

PASSENGER REGULAR

500 YEAR COMMEMORATIVE

FEDERAL GOVT.
VEHICLE

EMERGENCY
VEHICLE

BUS

AMATEUR RADIO

PLATE VALIDATION

MO/YR   MO/YR

FRONT PLATE   REAR PLATE

YEAR EXPIRE 02

YEAR EXPIRE 03

www.gov.nf.ca/wst

Newfoundland introduced the graphic plates(viking ship logo) in 1993, which will be phased in for all vehicles. Older plates. on issue since 1982, will continue to be used indefinitely. A limited edition "Cabot"commemorative plate is available for an additional fee.

Alpha prefixes with special meaning are:

CAA - CZZ - Commercial vehicle
BAA - BAZ - Bus
DAA - DAE - Dealer
EAA - EAZ - Emergency vehicle
FAA - FZZ - Farm, forestry,mining
GFA - GFZ - Federal government vehicle
GPA - GPZ - Provincial government

GMA - GMZ - Municipal government
MHA - Member of House Assembly
PRP - Prorated vehicle
TAA - TZZ - Trailer
TX - Taxi
W - Wrecker
XAA -XAZ - Construction equipment

Newfoundland & Labrador
Motor Registration Division, PO Box 8710
St. John's NF A1B 4J6   Tel. 709-729-2509

NOVA SCOTIA

2 PLATES VALIDATED
BY 2 DECALS
ON BOTH PLATES

DRIVER'S LICENSE

MOTORCYCLE

PASSENGER
(OLD SERIES)

PASSENGER AND
LIGHT COMMERCIAL

PERSONALIZED

HANDICAPPED

PRORATE VEHICLE

HEAVY (OVER 5000 kg)
COMMERCIAL

TRAILER

FIREFIGHTER

NEW VEHICLE DEALER

PLATE VALIDATION

YEAR EXPIRE 02

YEAR EXPIRE 03

NS

www.gov.ns.ca

All Nova Scotia plates are used for many years and revalidated by decals. Passenger plates have 3 alpha - 3 numeric characters and have no codes. The most recent issue is (Schooner "Bluenose"), however older passenger plates are still on the road. Heavy trucks, trailers and other commercial vehicles over 5000 Kg. have black on yellow. Government vehicle plates are black on beige, and prorated plates red on yellow. The alpha prefixes reserved for special use:

D -New car dealer)
F over M - Farm /fisherman truck)
F over T - Farm tractor
F over F(suffix)-Firefighter
G over T - General tractor

PR -Prorated
P over T - Semi-trailer
R - Government
T - Trailer
U - Used car dealer
VE1-Amateur radio

Nova Scotia Department of Transportation
Registry of Motor Vehicles, 6061 Young St
Halifax, NS B3J 2Z3

ONTARIO

2 PLATES VALIDATED BY 1 DECAL
ON REAR PLATE OF PASSENGER
AND FRONT PLATE OF
COMMERCIAL VEHICLES

DRIVER'S LICENSE

MOTORCYCLE

PASSENGER REGULAR
3 ALPHA - 3 NUMERIC

FEDERAL GOVERNMENT

PERSONALIZED

DIPLOMATIC CORPS.

ONTARIO GOVERNMENT

MEMBERS OF HOUSE
OF COMMONS

SENATOR

DEALER

AMATEUR RADIO

PLATE VALIDATION

MO/YR

FRONT PLATE	REAR PLATE	YEAR EXPIRE 02	YEAR EXPIRE 03	ON
		Decal colors change quarterly	Decal colors change quarterly	www.mto.gov.on.ca/

Most Ontario license plates have 6 or 7 characters divided by a crown.
Special plates are available in Ontario.

Arts	Community	Environment	Government

Heritage	Novelity	College	Sports

Sports	Professional

Ontario Ministry of Transportation
Safety and Regulation Division, 1201 Wilson Ave. East Bldg.
Downsview ON, M3M 1J8   Tel. 1-800-auto-PL8

PRINCE EDWARD ISLAND

ONE PLATE, 2 DECALS
CONFEDERATION BRIDGE

DRIVER'S LICENSE

MOTORCYCLE

Province House plate

Amateur radio

PERSONALIZED

MEMBER OF LEGISLATURE

FIREFIGHTER

HEAVY TRUCK (4500kg)

PUBLIC VEHICLE

PRORATED VEHICLE

FORMER GRAPHIC

PLATE VALIDATION

MO/YR

REAR PLATE

YEAR
EXPIRE
02
PEI 01/02
004138

YEAR
EXPIRE
03
PEI 02/03
004138

www2.gov.pe.ca/

These alpha prefixes are reserved for special use:

Commercial Truck
DLR - Dealers
F- Farm vehicle
FD- Firefighter
G - Government service
M - Motorcycle
PV - Public vehicle
SBA to **SBB**- School bus
SV - Service vehicle
SNOWMOBILE
OFF HIGHWAY

T- Trailer
TV-1/3 year heavy truck
VY2 - Ham radio call letters
XM- Citizens band radio

Prince Edward Island
Department of Transportation
PO Box 2000, Charlottetown, PEI C1A 7NS
Tel. 902-368-5200

QUEBEC

1 PLATE , QUEBEC NO LONGER
VALIDATES PLATES
WITH DECALS ON PLATES

DRIVER'S LICENSE

MOTORCYCLE

HANDICAPPED PERSON
WHEELCHAIR STICKER
UPPER RT. HAND CORNER

COMMERCIAL VEHICLE

RESTRICTED TRAVEL PLATE
(COLLECTOR VEHICLE)

TRUCK

TRUCK PERMANENT PLATE

TRUCK PRORATED

DEALER

BUS

CONSULAR OFFICIAL

PLATE VALIDATION

NO VALIDATION DECALS USED	YEAR EXPIRE 00 NO VALIDATION DECALS USED	YEAR EXPIRE 01 NO VALIDATION DECALS USED	QC

www.gov.qc.ca/

Quebec license plates all use the same design. Passenger plates are 3 alpha- 3 numeric and have no hidden codes. Other categories of plates have an alpha prefix which identifies the class and numerics that identifies the particular vehicle. All Quebec license plates are permanent.

A - Buses: Public, private, school
C - Vehicles with restricted right of travel.
CC - Consular corps
CD - Diplomatic Corps
F - Commercial vehicles
R - Trailers
T - Urban taxi

TR - Rural taxi
TS - Limousine
L - General merchandise transport
V - All terrain
VE2 - Ham radio
X - Dealer license plate.

Societe de l'assurance automobile du Quebec
333 Boulevard Jean-Lesage, C.P.19600
Quebec, PQ G1K 8J6
Tel. 418-528-3230

SASKATCHEWAN

2 PLATES VALIDATED BY CLASS
OF VEHICLE DECAL ON LOWER LEFT
AND YEAR DECAL LOWER RIGHT

DRIVER'S LICENSE

MOTORCYCLE

LT. GOVERNOR

MEDICAL DOCTOR

PERSONALIZED

DISABLED

COMMERCIAL TRUCK

FARM TRUCK

GOVERNMENT

COMMERCIAL TRAILER

LEASED VEHICLE

PLATE VALIDATION

DAY   MO/YR

FRONT PLATE   REAR PLATE

YEAR EXPIRE 02

SASK JAN 02

YEAR EXPIRE 03

SASK JAN 03

www.gov.sk.ca/

Saskatchewan license plates have 6 characters, 3 alpha- 3 numeric with a graphic wheat design separating the two groupings. The only exception is personalized and disabled person plates which have different character configurations and the wheat does not appear.. Different color alpha coded stickers are used to indicate the class of vehicle:

Green on White stickers
PV   - Private vehicle
T   - Private trailer
GC   - Government veh.
Blue on White Stickers
A   - Commercial
AG   - Public serv.veh
       restricted use.

C   - Commercial /
       restricted
D   - Commercial/
       provincial
TS   - Commercial
       trailer
L   - Leased
LT   - Leased trailer

PB   - Public bus
PC   - City bus
PS   - School bus
PT   - Public taxi
TS   - Commercial
       trailer
Red on White
F   - Farm

Saskatchewan Auto Fund
Government Insurance
2260 11th Ave., Regina, SK S4P 2N7
Tel. 306-787-4032

NORTHWEST TERRITORIES & NUNAVUT

2 PLATES VALIDATED BY 2 DECALS

DRIVER'S LICENSE

MOTORCYCLE

Nunavut 2 plates

COMMERCIAL

PUBLIC SERVICE (TRUCK)

GOVERNMENT OWNED VEHICLE

DEALER

RENTAL VEHICLE

TRAILER

AMATEUR RADIO

SCHOOL BUS

PLATE VALIDATION

DAY   MO/YR

REAR PLATE

YEAR EXPIRE **02**

YEAR EXPIRE **03**

NWT NU

All Northwest Territories and Nunavut plates are in the shape of a polar bear. Regular passenger vehicle plates are all numeric and the numbers have no other significance other than to identify the individual vehicle.Nunavut plates have an N suffix. Commercial, government and other vehicle plates have a 1 alpha prefix code:

N.W.T does not issue special plates to disabled persons.

C - Commercial Vehicle
D - Dealer
E - Public service vehicle (exempt)
G - Government owned vehicle

P - Public service vehicle (truck)
R - Rental vehicle (Hertz etc.)
S - School bus
T -Trailer   **VE8** - Ham radio

NORTHWEST TERRITORY DEPT. OF TRANSPORTATION
MOTOR VEHICLE DIVISION
PO BOX 1320, YELLOWKNIFE, NWT XJA 2L9
Tel. 403-667-8633

NUNAVUT
DIV. OF MOTOR VEHICLES
PO BOX 207
GJOA HAVEN, Nunavut
XOE150
867-360-6339

YUKON TERRITORY

1 PLATE VALIDATED BY
2 DECALS

DRIVER'S LICENSE

MOTORCYCLE

PERSONALIZED
2 PLATES ISSUED

ROYAL CDN
MTD POLICE

YUKON TERRITORIAL
GOVERNMENT

FEDERAL GOVERNMENT

RENTAL VEHICLE

LIGHT COMMERCIAL VEHICLE

HEAVY COMMERCIAL VEHICLE

DEALER

PLATE VALIDATION

MONTH   YEAR

REAR PLATE

YEAR EXPIRE 02
234567

YEAR EXPIRE 03
234567

www.gov.yk.ca/

Yukon Territory passenger plates have 3 alpha - 1 or 2 numeric characters. They have no codes. However the renewal month is assigned by the first initial of the owner's last name or the first letter of a corporate name.Other classes of vehicles can be identified by the alpha prefix on the plate:

C - Commercial
D,DLR - Dealer
F - Farm
G, YTG - Yukon Government
M - Motorcycle, moped
R - Rented vehicle
S - Snowmobile
T - Trailer
VE9- Ham radio call letters

First letter of name / word	Renew Mo.
F or H	January
M	February
B	March
D,V,O or E	April
N or T	May
W, Y, or R	July
K,J, or I	August
C, Q, or X	September
A or P	October
S,U, or Z	November
G or L	December

Yukon Territory
Community & Transportation Services
PO Box 2703, 308 Steele St.
White Horse, YT Y1A 2C6   Tel. 403-667-570203

123

MEXICO

States of Mexico

1. Aguascalientes (AGS)
2. Baja California (BC)
3. Baja California Sur (BCS)
4. Campeche (CAMP)
5. Chiapas (CHIS)
6. Chihuahua (CHIH)
7. Coahuila (COAH)
8. Colima (COL)
9. Durango (DGO)
10. Federal District (Mexico City) (DF)
11. Guanajuato (GTO)
12. Guerrero (GRO)
13. Hildago (HGO)
14. Jalisco (JAL)
15. Mexico (MEX)
16. Michoachan (MICH)
17. Morelos (MOR)
18. Nayarit (NAY)
19. Nuevo Leon (NL)
20. Oaxaca (OAX)
21. Puebla (PUE)
22. Queretaro (QRO)
23. Quintana Roo (QR)
24. San Luis Potosi (SLP
25. Sinaloa (SIN)
26. Sonora (SON)
27. Tabasco (TAB)
28. Tamaulipas (TAMPS)
29. Tlaxcala (TLAX)
30. Veracruz (VER)
31. Yucatan (YUC)
32. Zacatecas (ZAC)

Mexico issues 2 license plates to passenger vehicles. The authorit
provide a small decal of the exact plate which is attached to the windshi
as security measure.The states that border USA (BC, SON, CHIH. COA
and TAMPS) have a distinctive yellow FRONTERA license plate
vehicles that operate within 20 miles of the border. All private passeng
cars have traditionally had the same design- 3 or 4 letters and numbe
most recently green on white. The letters and numbers are issued
series within the state.But starting in 1998 distinctive graphics pla
began to appear... These colorful new plate designs seen on the hig
ways is positive evidence of the variety of culture and change in the sta
of modern Mexico. The spotting of the different license plates of Mexico
a favorite activity for travelers of all ages. We include a selection of the
new and old plate designs for your "collecting" enjoyment.

MEXICO (PRIVATE AUTO PLATES SHOWN EXCEPT WHERE INDICATED)

Aguascalientes

Baja California

Baja California
FRONTERA

Baja California Sur
Trailer

Campeche

Campeche
Taxi

Chiapas

Coahuila

Coahuila
FRONTERA

Chihuahua

Chihuahua
FRONTERA

Colima

Distrito Federal

Durango
Truck

Guanajuato

Auto Collector DF

Auto Collector
Pue

MEXICO

Guerrero

Hidalgo

Jalisco

Mexico

Michoacan

Morelos

Nayrit
Truck

Nuevo Leon

Nuevo Leon

Oaxaca

Oaxaca

Puebla Trailer

Queretaro

Quintana Roo

San Luis Potosi

Sinaloa

Sinaloa

Sonora

MEXICO

Sonora Frontera

Tabasco

Tamaulipas

Tamaulipas

Tamaulipas
Truck

Tamaulipas
Frontera

Tlaxcala

Tlaxcala

Veracurz

Veracruz

Yuz

Zacatecas

Zacatecas
Truck

**Auto Collector
Puebla**

Ambulance

NASCAR® special plates available to New York registered vehicles.

#1 Steve Park

Nascar® Regular Plate
numbers assigned as issued

#2 Rusty Wallace

Nascar® Regular Plate
numbers assigned as issued

#3 Dale Earnhardt

Nascar® Regular Plate
numbers assigned as issued

#6 Mark Martin

Nascar® Regular Plate
numbers assigned as issued

#3 Dale Earnhardt Jr

Nascar® Regular Plate
numbers assigned as issued

#18 Bobby Labonte

Nascar® Regular Plate
numbers assigned as issued

#20 Tony Stewart

Nascar® Regular Plate
numbers assigned as issued

#24 Jeff Gordon

Nascar® Regular Plate
numbers assigned as issued

#28 Ricky Rudd

NASCAR personalized plate
6 caracters of owners choice

#88 Dale Jarrett

NASCAR REGULAR

More plates coming soon.. #5, 11, 12, 15, 17,
19, 21, 22, 25, 29, 42, 43, 45, 97 and 99.

#2 Rusty Wallace

Nascar® Regular Plate
numbers assigned as issued

#3 Dale Earnhartdt

Nascar® Regular Plate
numbers assigned as issued

#6 Mark Martin

Nascar® Regular Plate
numbers assigned as issued

#8 Dale Earnhardt Jr

Nascar® Regular Plate
numbers assigned as issued

#17 Matt Kenseth

NASCAR personalized plate
6 caracters of owners choice

#2 Rusty Wallace

NASCAR personalized plate
6 caracters of owners choice

#3 Dale Earnhartdt

NASCAR personalized plate
6 caracters of owners choice

#6 Mark Martin

NASCAR personalized plate
6 caracters of owners choice

#8 Dale Earnhardt Jr

NASCAR personalized plate
6 caracters of owners choice

NASCAR®

NASCAR personalized plate
6 caracters of owners choice

#24 Jeff Gordon

Nascar® Regular Plate
numbers assigned as issued

#28 Ricky Rudd

Nascar® Regular Plate
numbers assigned as issued

#88 Dale Jarrett

Nascar® Regular Plate
numbers assigned as issued

#99 Jeff Burton

Nascar® Regular Plate
numbers assigned as issued

#24 Jeff Gordon

NASCAR personalized plate
6 caracters of owners choice

#28 Ricky Rudd

NASCAR personalized plate
6 caracters of owners choice

#88 Dale Jarrett

NASCAR personalized plate
6 caracters of owners choice

#99 Jeff Burton

NASCAR personalized plate
6 caracters of owners choice

More plates coming soon..
#18 Bobby Lanbonte
20 Tony Stewert
29 Kevin Harvick

DO YOU COLLECT LICENSE PLATES?

To Join A.L.P.C.A., The automobile License Plate Collectors Associati[c]

Write to:

A.L.P.C.A., INC.
7365 Main Street, #214
Stratford, CT 06614

You can visit their website at **WWW.ALPCA.ORG**

LICENSE PLATE GAMES

Motorists have discovered license plate spotting games are a great activity to help pass long hours on the highway. Make up your own rules, everyone can play, and all you need is a good pair of eyes, and maybe a pad and pencil. And as a word of advice, make it clear in the beginning that the driver is the final judge in all disputes - - exactly like the captain of a ship at sea!

Easy games:

Identify colors on a plate, find letters of the alphabet and numbers in sequence. Pick a "magic" two digit number or initials to see on a plate. Another variation is to pick a color and only the plates on that color vehicle "count".

Competitive games(fun for all ages):

SPELL THE SHORTEST WORD - Use the letters on a plate in the sequence they appear, and by adding letters construct the shortest word possible. Example : MLN-123 makes **M**ain**L**in**E** (8 letters) while **M**e**L**o**N** wins with 5 letters.

POKER- The first three numbers on the first plate you see is the start of your hand. Using the first two numbers on the next plate you have a basic poker hand. Make your wager, declare your discards (up to 3 numbers) and watch the next plate to draw your final hand. A variation is to use truck five digit plates.

DICE - Use the first number or numbers on a plate to determine dice combinations. If the first digits are 2 - 9, 11,12 use as is. If it is 13 - 19 add them together. For example13 becomes 4 (1+3). The first plate you see is your "roll". If the roll is 7 or 11 you win; 2 or 3 you lose; 12 you lose but keep your turn going first. All other possible sums (4,5,6,8,9,10) is your "point". To win, you must see your "Point" as the first numbers on a plate before one that begins with 7 or 16 which is the same as 7.

BLAZE A TRAIL - The object of this game is to "Blaze a trail" from coast to coast or between any two points of your choice- perhaps between New Jersey and Arizona if that is the destination of the trip. Look for license plates from states that border each other until you have a trail that connects your two points. Players take turns with time limits, or have only certain color vehicles to choose from. One rule is you must see a plate of a state that borders one you have seen to continue your "trail". You cannot see a plate out of sequence and "save" it for future use.

One last thought; make the person "spotting" a plate name the capital of the state or province before they can claim it in any game.

State/Province Checklist

Alabama	AL_____	North Carolina	NC_____
Alaska	AK_____	North Dakota	ND_____
Arizona	AZ_____	Ohio	OH_____
Arkansas	AR_____	Oklahoma	OK_____
California	CA_____	Oregon	OR_____
Colorado	CO_____	Pennsylvania	PA_____
Connecticut	CT_____	Rhode Island	RI_____
Delaware	DE_____	South Carolina	SC_____
Dist. Columbia	DC_____	South Dakota	SD_____
Florida	FL_____	Tennessee	TN_____
Georgia	GA_____	Texas	TX_____
Hawaii	HI_____	Utah	UT_____
Idaho	ID_____	Vermont	VT_____
Illinois	IL_____	Virginia	VA_____
Indiana	IN_____	Washington	WA_____
Iowa	IA_____	West Virginia	WV_____
Kansas	KS_____	Wisconsin	WI_____
Kentucky	KY_____	Wyoming	WY_____
Louisiana	LA_____		
Maine	ME_____	**CANADA**	
Maryland	MD_____	Alberta	AB_____
Massachusetts	MA_____	British Columbia	BC_____
Michigan	MI_____	Manitoba	MB_____
Minnesota	MN_____	New Brunswick	NB_____
Mississippi	MS_____	Newfoundland	NF_____
Missouri	MO_____	Northwest Terr.	NWT_____
Montana	MT_____	Nova Scotia	NS_____
Nebraska	NE_____	Nunavut	NU_____
Nevada	NV_____	Ontario	ON_____
New Hampshire	NH_____	Prince Edward Island	PEI_____
New Jersey	NJ_____	Quebec	QC_____
New Mexico	NM_____	Saskatchewan	SK_____
New York	NY_____	Yukon	YT_____

The Official License Plate Book 2002 Edition	$20.00
The License Plate Game	$ 5.00
Road Sign Game	$ 5.00
The License Plate Game on CD-ROM	$20.00
License Plate Quick-Check 2002	$ 2.00

Orders will be shipped postpaid to continental USA only.
Postage is extra for all Canadian and foreign orders .
Payment must be made with US dollars on US bank or credit card.

To order call toll free 1-800-347-0473

OR

send check or money order to:

Interstate Directory Publishing Company
220 Cleft Road,
Mill Neck, NY 11765.
Fax orders to 516-922-6605.

Visit us at our website IDPUBCO.COM for more information.

Publications From Interstate Directory Publishing Company

The Official License Plate Book 2002 Edition	$20.00
The License Plate Game	$ 5.00
Road Sign Game	$ 5.00
The License Plate Game on CD-ROM	$20.00
License Plate Quick-Check 2002	$ 2.00

Orders will be shipped postpaid to continental USA only.
Postage is extra for all Canadian and foreign orders .
Payment must be made with US dollars on US bank or credit car

To order call toll free 1-800-347-0473

OR

send check or money order to:

Interstate Directory Publishing Company
220 Cleft Road,
Mill Neck, NY 11765.
Fax orders to 516-922-6605.

Visit us at our website IDPUBCO.COM for more information.